NOMADS (

personal

the university of arizona press

TUCSON

photographs & interviews by barbara seyda

NOMADS OF A DESERT CITY

stories from citizens of the street

The University of Arizona Press
© 2001 Barbara Seyda
First Printing

⊛ This book is printed on acid-free, archival-quality paper.
Manufactured in the United States of America

06   05   04   03   02   01   6   5   4   3   2   1

The interviews conducted for this documentary project took place during 1998 and 1999. Each narrative was recorded and transcribed as oral history and has not been researched, investigated, verified, or confirmed as truthful or factual. The texts in this book are life stories as related by each participating individual.

Library of Congress Cataloging-in-Publication Data
Seyda, Barbara, 1957–
Nomads of a desert city : personal stories from citizens of the street / photographs and interviews by Barbara Seyda.
p. cm.
ISBN 0-8165-2077-1 (cloth : alk. paper) —
ISBN 0-8165-2079-8 (paper : alk. paper)
1. Homeless persons—Arizona—Tucson—Biography.
2. Homeless persons—Arizona—Tucson—Portraits.
3. Tucson (Ariz.)—Social conditions. I. Title.
HV4506.T83 S49 2001
305.5′69—dc21
2001000366

British Library Cataloguing-in-Publication Data
A catalogue record for this book is available from the British Library.

for samuel, my friend and inspiration

contents

Preface ix

Acknowledgments xi

1. Byrdy Wood 2

2. "Pa Kettle" 10

3. Dorothy Stout 18

4. Doug McClellan 26

5. LaManda Long 32

6. Delores Johnson 38

7. Samuel Manuel Hernandez Martinez 46

8. Deanna Gillingham 54

9. Glenn Kiyota 60

10. Vivian Corbett 68

11. Jon Paul Ferlan 76

12. "Sweet Forgetfulness" 84

13. Steve Anton Kati 92

Resource Guide 99

According to the National Coalition for the Homeless, a growing shortage of affordable housing, an increase in the number of people living in poverty, the lack of affordable health care, domestic violence, and chemical dependency are responsible for the rise in homelessness. Many homeless people are fully employed but cannot afford an apartment. Some homeless people suffer from a mental illness or physical disability. Almost half of homeless men are veterans of war. And when a woman leaves an abusive spouse, she and her children very often automatically become homeless.

I became interested in this book project documenting stories and portraits of homeless people when I moved to the Armory Park neighborhood in downtown Tucson several years ago. I was struck by how many homeless people walked down our street each day. Sometimes as many as fifty or sixty people pushed carts, hauled bags of belongings, peered into garbage cans, or sat against brick walls drinking or smoking cigarettes. Many were en route to local soup kitchens or agencies offering coffee, laundry facilities, a phone, clothes, blankets, or a free meal.

According to Lynn Ratener of the Tucson Planning Council for the Homeless, there are 2,600 to 3,200 people without a home in Tucson. I met many of the people featured in this book in the downtown area. They are old and young, and of all ethnic, educational, and cultural backgrounds. During the interview process, some revealed that they did not consider themselves to be "homeless" at all. They identified a "home" as any place where they located themselves, a sanctuary of sorts. It could be a piece of sidewalk, a sewer, a corner, an arroyo, a cardboard box, or a chair.

How to define the concept of "home" was just one of many complex issues that emerged during this project. Each story contains insights, questions, and uncertainties. A face sometimes reveals what words cannot. Here are thirteen people I met. These stories and portraits are their forgotten lives and faces.

acknowledgments

This book was made possible through the generous philanthropic support of the following individuals: Kristie Graham, Alice Belmont, George and Harriet-Karr McDonald of the Doe Fund, John and Alice Seyda, Lisa and Pam Liberty-Bibbens, Andrew Silverman, and Mary Goodman.

I am grateful for the vision and enthusiasm of Patti Hartmann, my editor, who believed in this project from the first moment I walked into her office. Many thanks to Karen Uhlich, Kate Hiller, and Jennifer Boyett of Primavera Services; Betty Eppler of Casa Paloma; Mary Pat Sullivan of Comin' Home; and English Gama of the Cooperative Outreach Project on AIDS in Southern Arizona (COPASA) for their high spirit of cooperation and for giving this project its momentum. For executing beautiful prints, a big thank you to Keith Schreiber and Photographic Works. And I thank Bill Reisner for his legal counsel.

For their collaborative effort and support, I would like to thank my wonderful team at the University of Arizona Press: Christine Szuter, Director; Anne Keyl, Design and Production Manager; Judith Allen, Managing Editor; Kathryn Conrad, Marketing Manager; Tappan King, Publicity Manager; and Annie Barva, Manuscript Editor. And special thanks to Lisa Bowden for her impeccable book design.

I'd also like to extend a heartfelt thanks to my sister M. J., whose work within the homeless community encouraged me to pursue this project. Many thanks to Deborah Wozniak, friend and colleague, for precise feedback and insight. For invaluable patience, inspiration, and support, I also thank my life partner, Diana Herrera.

My deepest appreciation, however, goes to all of the individuals whom I interviewed and photographed, for their willingness to be seen and heard and felt.

byrdy wood

rainbow planet café

Byrdy was hanging out at the
Rainbow Planet when I met her on a
saturday afternoon. I was there
to get a mango smoothie, and she
was waiting for a ride to a rave
in phoenix. Her long blonde hair
was clipped with multicolored,
heart-shaped barrettes, her nose
and tongue were pierced, and she
was wearing green army fatigues
and sneakers. A quiet grunge kid
with deep brown eyes, she had
slept for only an hour the pre-
vious night. Although tired and
impatient, she sat with me at a
small table and agreed to tell
her story.

I'm seventeen years old.

I was married in a little hotel room in Anchorage, Alaska. I was really drunk. It was three days before my fifteenth birthday. My ex-husband was nineteen when we got married. We met in a shelter in Alaska. It was an interesting experience. I learned a lot from it, but it was a pretty bad situation. I was depressed and trying to do the best I could. He was doing what he felt he needed to do at the time, but I cared about me and my daughter. My daughter will be a year and a half next month on the eleventh of June. She's in Alaska with my mom right now. I didn't want her out on the street with me. It didn't seem right to have a child out on the streets. My ex-husband is her father. I'm divorced now. Yeah, it was for the best.

I was born in L.A. County, California, February 11, 1982. I have one brother that's now fifteen, and a sister that's three years old. My mom's Scandinavian. My dad's like a mixture, like Scottish, Irish, German, and Dutch. My mom works as a janitor at a high school in Glen Allen, Alaska. My dad's an engineer in California. I was four when they divorced. My mom got full custody of me.

I've been living on the streets on and off for about three years. I ran away from home because of my mom's boyfriend. I really did not care for him at all. He's a good guy, but has problems. I still refuse to go home because of him. He was an alcoholic. Now he's actually recovering from the alcohol. I feel I got thrown out because of that situation. It's hard to discuss things with my mom. There's an ongoing tension between us. I'm not sure if she wants to acknowledge it. She always loves me and continues to say, "Will you please come back up here?" But her boyfriend and I don't get along. And, like, I don't want that situation around me because I was an alcoholic about three years back, and I don't want to go back to it.

I was twelve when I started drinking. I drank anything. I drank because I was bored. There was nothing better to do in Alaska. I was pretty much just trying to hang out with my friends. I lived in a little native village, about two hundred miles from any major city in Alaska. There's like two hundred people in my village. Athabaskan, Aleut, Tlingit, and Haida. We were one of the few white families. I finished middle school but I didn't make it through the ninth grade.

I went back to Highland High School in Albuquerque at the beginning of the school year for like three and a half weeks, but I had to quit because my ex-husband didn't have a job. We had like no money for rent.

He wasn't taking care of the baby, so I had to take control and like fix the problem.

I was arrested by the police for being a runaway in Anchorage and moved back with my mom. When my mom came to see me and pick me up, I convinced her to let me stay in Anchorage with my husband. We lived there for a month because we couldn't afford an apartment anymore. It was eight hundred dollars for a cheap motel room for a month. It was really, really hard to live there, to survive easily, so we went with my mom for a month. Then her boyfriend ended up getting drunk one night and kicking down the door and starting this huge fight over me baby-sitting my baby sister. And like a week and a half later, I was on a plane to California.

When I got to California, my dad couldn't support me. My dad tried really hard, but I didn't want to leave my boyfriend. My dad lives with my grandparents. My grandmother and my grandfather were strong focal points of support for me through my childhood. When I had hard times, they were always there for me. But my dad works hard and struggles. It's hard for him. He had no place for me to live. Especially not with a husband. My ex-husband's parents said they would take care of us if we came into town. When we got into town, to Albuquerque, they said, "Get lost!"

Tonight I'm going to Phoenix for a rave. Then I'd like to go to Albuquerque. I have a lot of friends there. I lived there for two years, before I came here. The guy who drove me out here refused to take me back to Albuquerque. So he's like, "You can either travel with me, or you can get out here in Tempe, or you can wait 'til we get to Tucson and find somebody to, like, take care of you there." I was like, "I'll wait 'til Tucson." That was the first week in December.

I first was squatting in like tunnels and hotel rooms with other people. And then I like moved into a camper with some friends. And I got arrested. They put me in jail for two days, and then they put me in a group home for a month. I got arrested for trespassing because I was down in the tunnels one night visiting some friends because they were leaving town. I was arrested because they had a "No Trespassing" sign there. We just didn't notice it. We didn't really know it was illegal, anyway.

I was in a group home for one month and moved to an independent living program, and I stayed there for five or six days. Then I moved back into the trailer. I stayed there for about a month and a half. Then I moved into a friend's apartment, and I stayed there for a few weeks until she kicked me out because she went psycho. She was like pregnant and not a good person to be around when she's pregnant. So I ended up back out here, and now I'm kind of floating around. I'm going to leave for Albuquerque because I'm tired of it. I'm tired of like the same thing happening. I just want to go, try something else.

I ask for spare change if I really have to. I ask friends to buy me stuff if I need to. There's other things I do. I like don't prostitute myself or anything like that. I refuse to do anything like that, but I have resorted to drug dealing before. I'm using marijuana. That's about it. I used to do a lot of LSD. Kids should stay away from too many chemical drugs, especially meth, coke, crack, and heroine. A little bit of LSD here and there really doesn't hurt too much. It does hurt, but if you feel you can handle it, go for it.

In the next few years, I just want to be able to have my kid and like either have like a house to live in or something or, like, a really nice camper or a van and go traveling with my kid. Show her what I can of the world. She likes traveling. She likes going out to the mountains and camping. Going new places. She likes meeting new people. I thought that might be fun for her if we traveled.

What I'd like people to understand is that most of us are *kind* kids. We're not going to go and rob you or, like, go and hold you up for your money or pickpocket you. I've had so many people, when I was spare-changing, like I'd turn around and look at them, and they are holding their wallets as they walk away. It makes me feel so pathetic and disgraced to see that. You know, some of us have been trying to survive. Some people say the youth of America is going to take over, but, yet, we're the youth of America, and nobody cares about us. Not many people. I mean, they shun us. They look down on us. Just act like we don't even exist. When I ask people for spare change out on the streets, and they don't even acknowledge that I'm there, it makes me so mad. They could at least say, "No, have a nice day."

I've experienced discrimination. I've been thrown out of places because I'm homeless—like [restaurants], places like that. I have been physically threatened. I've been molested by about four different people while

I've been out on the streets. One was kind of a stranger to me. I didn't know all of them very well. But like, the other three were people that I did trust. They were people on the street. I wasn't raped. I always stopped it before it got to that point.

Right now, I'm afraid of everything. It's just I have to remember that I need the strength to continue on Earth; otherwise I'm not going to last. My daughter won't have a mom. I miss her a lot. She's like the one that keeps me going. The last time I saw her was in November.

Quite a few people have made a difference in my life. Like Donna Rowe in Albuquerque. She's the director of Youth in Transition. It's a homeless program that takes in all the hard-core street kids that have like been rejected by all the other programs or can't access them for one reason or another. I haven't really been rejected, but the shelter system does not work for me. It just really doesn't because they focus on what they want their goals to be. They don't focus on what I want my goals to be.

My goal is to survive. And get my daughter back.

pa kettle (wesley ernest bryan) rides a purple, three-wheel bike that carries one loaf of bread, a bible, incense, a frying pan, camp stove, propane, and blankets. I first heard pa on the library plaza playing a xylophone, which he had constructed with chimes, old pieces of wood, and string. Always elegantly dressed in suspenders, button-down shirt, and hat, pa has five children and eight grandchildren. sitting nearby was his wife of more than thirty-six years, ma kettle, who grew up on the upper west side in manhattan.

where and when was I born?

Born in St. Louis, Missouri, 1935. I have four brothers and five sisters. My parents were born in Haiti, and my grandfather was born in Haiti. We moved back to Haiti when I was twelve 'til I was sixteen. I worked in the cane fields. See, down South, people chop cotton. Over there, people do sugar cane. Then we had to leave again. See, my grandfather was a voodoo witch doctor. When he became saved, he got ran out of Haiti for it. That's why we had to leave. Then he got over here, and he had to eat, so he got into the rackets.

See, my grandfather ran liquor and cigarettes. He sold 'em on the streets for folks. Yes, that's what he done. My grandfather worked for a guy in New York called Bumpy Johnson. He was like a big-time black gangster in New York. See, I go back, like the old-timers. We like to say, "Back in our day, we had real gangsters. We all wore suits. None of this baseball cap stuff." (Laughs.) But it's pretty much the same program. See, back then, before they came up with the Federal Stamp Tax Act, you could go to North Carolina, get a truckload of cigarettes, and make a killin' in New York. That was the hustle back then. You know. It was a victimless crime.

At sixteen, I came back to St. Louis. I wanted to be a little gangster, so I got me a bunch of suits and hats, and I tried to hang out like the fellas on the block. See, when I was comin' up, you had to deal with the possibility of what was your role models. In our neighborhood, the guys in the suits always seemed to look better. They always seemed to have food on the table—even though they had a down side. They was always slippin' cops envelopes, and every now and then their little place would get kicked in. When I was comin' up, runnin' numbers was the big thing in our neighborhood, and I was a numbers runner. See, what they do now, they call it Powerball. It was the same thing we was doin', but it was illegal in our days.

My neighborhood was East St. Louis. Yes, Pruitt-Igoe. The worst projects in the country. They had to blow it up. (Laughs.) It was the first public-housing experiment in this country on a mass scale, but it got so bad in St. Louis, they had to blow it up in order to close it down because it just got crazy. They moved everybody out. They didn't really relocate. They gave everybody a little check and said, "Get out! Don't be here Monday when the wreckin' ball come in." (Laughs.)

Anytime they say "urban renewal," that mean "there goes the neighborhood." Somebody gettin' a parkin' lot. You know, it usually signals the destruction of the neighborhood. You felt protected by your neighborhood. If you needed anything, somebody in the neighborhood would hook you up. Now you don' have dat. Well, I do amongst a certain sober few out here. We call ourselves "street soldiers" because we all sober and we don't get no pop for it. We have to watch each other against everybody else. Some people would call us a gang, but we're not a gang. We don't smoke crack. We don't smoke weed. We don't drink. We just watch each other's butt. If somebody got to go to work, then somebody else will watch their stuff for 'em that day. See, that type of thing. If you don't have dat, you don't have no protection. If you leave your stuff somewhere, it's gone. You gotta watch yourself all the time. Four or five irate drunks'll kill each other over a sleeping bag. This is not the roughest camp. I've been in some rough camps. In Detroit, we had three buggies. We had two guns in each buggy. Needed it just to get through the various neighborhoods to get to the soup line. It's been that bad.

I've only been clean two years. Where was I livin' in New York? Behind Sardi's. Before that, I used to live in the tunnels. Remember when everyone was livin' down in the subway tunnels? I was stayin' in a tunnel right by the Port Authority, Thirty-fourth Street. They come in and ran everybody up out of there. Two o'clock in the morning. That's when I moved back to Sardi's. Eighteenth Street on the East Side. Yes. It's a big-time restaurant. It's super high society. A biscuit cost you fifty dollars. Yes. A glass of water would probably cost you about twelve dollars, and they want a tip when you leave. Yes. I wound up getting a job there, and that helped a lot. Took a lot of pressure off.

See, people can never really understand homelessness until they go through it, 'cause Americans have this problem: "As long as it's not one of my relatives and not in my backyard, I don't see it except on TV." You know? "I might catch it if it's on *Oprah*." You know? "If it happens to be on the nightly news and it's around Christmas time, I might dig in my drawer and find somethin' to give that po' homeless guy, so I can feel guilty before the tax write-off man comes." You know? (Laughs.) People never really understand until it actually happens to them.

When we was in New Orleans, this lady used to come down every weekend and throw eggs at the homeless. I don't mean physical eggs. I mean verbally: "Why don't you bums get a job?!" She was one of those high, city council–type people. Then when they had that flood and her house got wiped out, now she's one of the biggest outreach workers they got down there. Now she can't do enough for the homeless. Why? Because it took an act of God to get her off her high horse. You understand what I'm sayin'?

But they make big money off of you. All of the government organizations—the homeless industry. Most of it disappear in that little gray area called "operational overhead." You understand what I'm sayin'? They could do a lot more than what they're doing. They ain't that slow when it comes to building a prison! They can always seem to find prison room. Can't find no shelter, you know, buildings for battered and abused women. But they can always build a prison! You know, a lady gettin' beat up by her boyfriend. "Oh, we're sorry. We don't have bed space we got so many people." But they got that prison. Better go out and shoot that fool! You understand what I'm sayin'? It's all relative.

And what's the biggest thing now? What's the biggest thing now? Now, it's privatizing all of these institutions, so you absolutely have no rights. The ᴀᴄʟᴜ [American Civil Liberties Union] can't do nothin.' Have your rights been violated? What rights? You have no rights! The only rights you have out here is the class you carry within yourself. Those are the only real rights you have out here.

Just hope that you never go through it. This is none of that Jack Kerouac thing where everybody decides "let's go Beatnik around the country." This is crap. See, back then, it was a movement to change things around. Now it's just somethin' that happens to your butt. You can't control the circumstances, but you can control how you live and operate within those circumstances. There's nothin' romantic about it. You can go to jail out here just for bein' sleepy and tired. You can. You can be layin' up under that tree. Cop don't like you, you can go to jail for vagrancy or whatever he decides to come up with. In other words, just being honest, just being sober, just bein' safe ain't no guarantee that you ain't gonna get harassed.

When I'm playin' music, people come up and say, "Here's a buck." That may not be a lot to them, but to me it's a lot. Most of the time, when you give money to people on the street, you're participating in their genocide because you know they're going to go out and buy liquor. You know they're going to go out there and buy crack. When people come up and say, "I never see you drunk no more, here," "I know that you're really tryin', here," when somebody gives me money, they are helping with my liberation. Big difference. If I was strung out, then they would be participating in my genocide 'cause I'm actually fightin' not to die.

Another phenomenon now is a lot of people want to have shelters. A lot of people want to build soup lines and soup kitchens. All of sudden, there's a lot of government money out here. Everybody tryin' to do a shelter and become another movement hustler. You know? In order to get that tax bracket. You have to watch out for them. You get to know one or two people on the city council and get you a zone in the right neighborhood, and you can have you a nice lil' shelter *too*. That's another trend you have to watch out for 'cause it may start out all meaning well, but you start gettin' all that government money, people change, boy! People like Jim Bakker. Straight-up swindlers.

See, I am a dying breed: an honest bum in America. (Laughs.) I'm serious. You know, that's an enigma nowadays. You know? Politicians are crooked. Preachers are crooked. Cops are scary and crooked. You understand what I'm sayin'? Can't look to your leaders no more for leadership. Can't be a role model no more. You know? All the decent heroes and Lone Ranger croaked.

So what's left? Guys like me. See, at least when I go, God say, "Well, what have you got to say fo' yo'self?" I can say, "Yeah, I was a bum, but I was an honest bum. Run the tape." I ain't got to look over my shoulder. You understand? I did some really dumb stuff, which I pass on to the growin' up of my youth. But as I get older, I get straighter. So you can run this tape. At least I can go out like dat.

dorothy stout

casa paloma

In mid-january, Betty Eppler, executive director of the women's shelter casa Paloma, invited me for Monday-night dinner. Also known as the "pink house," casa paloma is a quiet refuge in Barrio Anita. In addition to housing for nine residents, it has a daily drop-in center and a huge city garden surrounded by magenta and pink hollyhocks. That night, I sat with the residents and ate jambalaya, black-eyed peas, corn bread, and brownies prepared for us by **Dorothy stout.** A resident at casa paloma for several months, Dorothy had decorated her small room with a wildflower poster she had hand colored with magic markers and a latch-hook rug of a desert scene.

Being asked to live here

was an honor for me. I've been here since July 6, 1998. It was real scary at first because I didn't know what was expected of me, and I didn't know if I would be okay enough to live in a situation like this. For the bed, they have a lot of applicants that come in. I know that I am real grateful for it because if I had to go back to my situation, I would have wound up in a mental hospital.

At this point, I consider this my home. It's really hard for women—especially if we're single women with a job. A lot of us women are just getting minimum wage. It's just really hard to take care of a car, an apartment, and all the necessities of life. Most of us are living paycheck to paycheck. If we don't get one or two paychecks, that would mean total homelessness.

My average day is pretty nice. I get up around seven fifteen. First thing I do is go out and smoke. Then I come in and take a shower and have coffee. I talk to the women in the house and say the "good mornings." I usually hang around until quarter to nine, and most of the time [a friend] and I catch the bus together. Once I'm at the Ronstadt [Transit Center], I catch my university bus and that takes me to work. I have a nice little walk from the bus stop to Park Place. I go in there and feel real good. I look forward to what I'm doing. It may seem menial, but it's just perfect for me at this time. I'm just a food-service worker—serving food to the students. I like the students. I like my co-workers. They're just wonderful. It's a happy atmosphere. I get through my four and half hours very nicely, serving students and faculty members. I start at ten. I get a fifteen-minute cigarette break, and I go back in and finish up. We set up the food, and then we take down the food at two o'clock. I work until half past two, then I run to get a bus home.

Right now, my greatest pleasure is just getting up in the morning and feeling good—feeling worthy, feeling that there is something to get up for. That's real nice. My biggest challenge is getting through the post-traumatic stress and dealing with the therapy that I have to go through, working on the *Courage to Heal* workbook. I'm just real tired of the past keeping me real sick and stagnant. As a child, I just have no idea how I survived. I'm working on these issues right now. The only thing I can say is if I made it through my childhood, I can make it through anything.

I was born in Trenton, New Jersey, in 1960. My dad is Spanish, but I've never met him. I have no memories of my real father at all. There was a picture hanging around that my grandmother had, but my mother found it and ripped it apart. My mother had me when she was very young. She was fifteen or sixteen. My mom is Pennsylvania Dutch. She was in Trenton when I was born, but I spent my childhood in different towns. My mother had worked all her life and still is, as far as I know. We had enough money to get by. There was money for extras. We didn't live in any place spectacular. It was a bunch of apartments, when I was a child. When I became an adolescent, we moved to Phillipsburg, New Jersey. I have two half-sisters, which were born when I was a preteen, so I was an only child from birth up until the age of eleven.

All my childhood memories are bad. Unfortunately, the only memories I have are of physical abuse and sexual abuse. My mother was verbally and physically abusive, and my first stepfather was sexually abusive, and my second stepfather was sexually abusive. The second one my mother stayed with the longest. I was four and a half when the sexual abuse began, and I was suicidal since the first time my stepfather sexually abused me. My first attempted suicide was when I was four and a half, right after the first incident. I had taken some rubbing alcohol and drank it, hoping to die from it. My mother found me and got very angry with me because she had to take me to the hospital to get my stomach pumped.

My mother was a rageaholic. She didn't do drugs. She only drank occasionally, but she was a daily rageaholic. She was very physically and verbally abusive. I was not her favorite child. She was highly critical, always told me I was stupid. She would yell if there was a little piece of lint on the floor. We didn't have much of a relationship at all.

My second stepfather got me pregnant my first year of high school, when I was fifteen, so I didn't make it through high school. I kept trying to go back, but it wasn't working. By the time I was fifteen, I was an alcoholic.

They wouldn't let me have an abortion. I was forced to go through the pregnancy. My stepfather was in denial. He blamed a cousin for that pregnancy. That's what he told my mother, and that's what he told my grandparents, so I was living with a lot of lies. During my pregnancy, there were a lot of suicide attempts. It was just miserable. My stepfather was sexually assaulting me during that pregnancy. In April of '76, I had the baby. It was a boy. My stepfather and my mother took care of him. My mother basically raised him. The child knows that I'm his biological mother, but my mother is the one that took care of him. I believe he knows who his father is. It would be difficult for him not to know because when he looks in the mirror, he looks just like my stepfather.

When I was nineteen, I met my husband. We didn't get married until I was twenty-three. Well, he liked to party like I did. We had that in common—and nothing else. We had two children. I chose to give them up when I was eighteen-months sober. I'm not maternal. I am my mother's child. I had a real hard time—even in recovery—taking care of the kids. They were born in 1986 and '88, and I got sober in '89. I had a son and a daughter. My mother-in-law, thank God for her, took the children a lot. She basically raised them. There was a lot of fear there because of the way I was raised, and I saw that I wasn't doing a real good job with them.

I'm divorced now. We finalized the divorce in '96. We haven't been together since '91. Right after [my second son] was born, I tried to get a place of our own, and I found out my husband had a major cocaine addiction, which I wasn't aware of. He was doing his thing, and I was trying to get our lives together, and it just wasn't happening.

In December of '95, I had a breakdown and wound up in the hospital. We found out that I had the winter blues and that winter triggers a lot of my post-traumatic stress, so I moved out here. My doctor recommended that I move here. I came out here by myself. I took the Greyhound bus. I gave up all my possessions back home. Moved out here with just a couple suitcases and a bag full of books. I sure remember that ride. It was really exciting. I felt really good. I felt for once in control of my life, and I wasn't scared of what would happen to me. I had managed to save up enough money to get an apartment, and I found a job within the first four days I moved out here [at] a little tiny nursing home, family-owned. I was an aide.

Around my apartment, there was too much noise. I had complained, and the complaints weren't being listened to. I had just broken up with my boyfriend and was getting very depressed. In March, I wound up sitting in the samhc [Southern Arizona Mental Health Center] office, and they sent me to one of the hospitals—I think it was Palo Verde Hospital. I did a ten-day stint there. Then they sent me to St. Joe's unit at the O'Rielly [Care]

Center [a short-term detox unit and psychiatric treatment center]. I wasn't even there twenty-four hours, and I had a suicide attempt due to the fact that the doctor they had given me looked just like my stepfather. That just took me back down. I wound up in Kino [county hospital] for twenty-four hours. Then the Carondelet [Health Network] system took over and sent me to St. Mary's—run by nuns. I was there for ten days at the psychiatric center. They put me on a bunch of hard medications and sent me home. Four days later I wound up back in St. Mary's Hospital again because of the medication they gave me. I was having bad hallucinations.

At the end of June, I wound up in the hospital again because I wasn't getting any better. I was getting near suicidal again. I wound up in PUF, which is at La Frontera [clinic], psychiatric-unit facility. This was last year. It was not a good year. PUF was really wonderful and found me a bed here. I've been here at Casa Paloma ever since.

I'm still feeling scarred over the way that my mother brought me up—the way that it still affects how I feel about myself today. It's been a major process for me to undo a lot of the negative tapes and switch them to positive ones. Judy, my therapist at La Frontera, has been a real positive help in this area. She won't let me get down on myself. She absolutely always finds something good in me, even when I can't. She's been prominent in my healing. Laura is my therapist at the Rape Crisis Center, and she's been great. We've come real far. Then this Friday I go to see my psychiatrist. I've been through several psychiatrists since I've been here.

Right now, it's just the little things that I'm doing—like affirmations—that help. I say thirty affirmations a night. They're highly repetitive. I'm saying the same things over and over. I am starting to get results. I also keep little cards around so I can tell myself that I need to take care of myself. One of my favorites is, "To be able to grace the world with my presence, I need to take care of myself."

This issue of sexual abuse has followed me most of my grown life. The alcohol covered it up when I was in my twenties, but when I got sober at twenty-nine, the issues really started coming up. The more time I had sober, the more severe the sexual abuse issues had gotten. For other women who have suffered sexual abuse, I do believe that we can recover from it, but we really need to take a look at what happened to us and be honest and realize that there was a problem. That's all I have to say.

doug mcclellan

Doug McClellan lives at the Alamo, a low-income, transitional housing program for men on Stone and Sixth Avenue in Tucson. A big guy wearing a baseball cap, sunglasses, and a Route 66 T-shirt, Doug was eating a sandwich when I met him on his lunch break at the employment office of Primavera Services, an organization that provides shelter, housing, employment opportunities, and relief to the homeless. Doug works fulltime on a cleanup crew, picking up trash in local parks and neighborhoods, where, he says, "he gets good exercise and works on his tan." Recently diagnosed with a brain tumor, Doug told me he was glad to "be here still, waking up every morning."

I was working back at the labor hall

up until August of last year, and I started feeling really bad. I was getting headaches, so I went to the doctor and got diagnosed with a growth in my head, which I'm taking medication for now. At that time, I was on the streets. I was sleeping under the third bush from the left, next to an arroyo, or camping out on the desert. I spent an awful lot of money to keep from getting headaches. I could barely concentrate on walking down the street. It kept on getting worse. I was losing weight.

Finally, I went to the hospital and go, "What's wrong?" I found out. It was benign cancer. It could have been just from doing drugs in college. I did anything you could imagine in any combination. I think I had over two hundred LSD trips, and I'm still able to think. The scan showed the growth is decreasing, which is good. This growth was about the size of my thumb, but it's shrinking. I still get the headaches, but they're not as bad. They gave me some medication last year which was suppressing the bone marrow function, so I was not making any red blood cells and was really anemic. I was in the hospital for fourteen days before Christmas. A normal blood count for hemoglobin is between 15 and 16, and mine was down to like 2.8, so I was barely walkin' around. But they switched the medication, and I'm doing much better.

I'm on AHCCCS now [Arizona Health Care Cost Containment System, a program that provides funding to the poor or people with no medical insurance]. I qualified for it after the fourteen-day hospital stay. It includes all my prescriptions, and if I have to go to the hospital again, it'll be covered. I pay for food, housing, and bus fare. Housing's a real good deal. At the Alamo, there are studio apartments where you pay $125 a month. My roommate works during the night, and I work during the day, so we don't see each other too often except on weekends. I've been living at the Alamo since the first of February. I was in the men's shelter for five months on East Benson Highway. I was sharing a warehouse-type building with 105 other guys. I'd been there off and on over the past eight years. I delivered all the plumbing supplies for that place when they first built it in '86. I used to work down at Guadalupe, Casa Maria, for awhile too. It's a soup kitchen. I used to make thirty gallons of soup a day.

I was raised on the Presbyterian work ethic. You had to work to keep a roof over your head and food in your stomach. Nobody was going to give you nothing. You had to go out and earn it. Doing something right, doing a job the right way is a pretty good reward in and of itself. I suppose it was my grandfather—a Presbyterian minister—who had an impact on me. I must have been listenin' when I was real young.

My childhood was pretty good. I was born the twelfth of June, 1949, in Lansing, Michigan. I have two brothers and one sister. Dad worked for General Motors, and my mother worked for a radio station. We were German Irish and Scotch. My dad's parents spoke nothing but Gaelic, and my mother's parents spoke nothing but German. I don't remember any of it. They were from Europe, but my parents were born here. I'm next to the youngest. I'm also the shortest one of the three guys. Me and my brothers were always playing sports all year round, no matter what time of year it was. Baseball, hockey, basketball, and football.

I suppose my grandfather had an impact on me, the more I think about it. He taught me how to be "tolerant"—to see the other person's point of view. He took us to a church in Lansing, and we heard Malcolm X talk back when he was still alive. I must have been in seventh or eighth grade. I thought it was pretty good 'cause he told everybody, "Hey, everybody's equal. If people don't treat you right, it's your duty and your obligation to stand up and say, 'Hey, you're not treating me right.'" This was the way I was brought up through our church, anyway. No matter what color of skin you had, everybody should be treated right. It's just the way it should be.

I went to Genessey Street Elementary School. High school was J. W. Sexton, rah rah! I graduated in 1967. I went to college for one year at Michigan State. I studied archaeology as my major and political science minor. When I first started out, I was living at home, and then I moved into my own place. Then I worked for the post office in Lansing for a year and a half. After that, I took classes but never got a degree. I just hung out, worked odd jobs. Mostly construction trade—carpentry, plumbing, electrical. In '73, after my dad died, I moved out here to Tucson and got my first job working for my uncle's topless bar.

One of my cousins was coming out, and he said, "You want to come out and work for your uncle in Tucson?" With my part of the inheritance, I said, "Well, sure." Change of scenery, 'cause I traveled a lot when I was in college. I hitchhiked out to Denver in the summertime and hitchhiked all around, so I wanted to see what Arizona was like.

I was a bartender and a bouncer at my uncle's bar. We used to get people calling up there to get their cars checked. "No, no, it's not that kind of a body shop." Actually, he had another bar down in Sierra Vista which was a totally nude bar. I'd have to drive the dancers between Tucson and Sierra Vista in this big ol' green-and-white Cadillac about once a month. Mostly, I made sure the guys didn't get too rowdy and try to paw the girls.

Then I got a job being a bouncer at a local rock 'n' roll bar down on Fourth Avenue. I worked there for three years and then at another bar down the street which was a punk-rock bar. That was interesting. Then on the fifth of June in 1983, [it] was deliberately set on fire. I happened to be inside of it at the time. The owner paid a friend of mine to burn it down, and they didn't know I was going to be in there at the time. I was sitting in the office reading *The Autobiography of Joseph Bonanno*. I smelled the smoke and got out. It didn't take long for it to burn at all. It was made of old barn wood. Went up real quick.

I was staying at the bar, some quarters upstairs from the bar. I moved out and moved in with my girlfriend I had at the time. Found out her ex-husband had burnt down her duplex. I walked in the door one day, and the fire investigator and firefighter were sitting there talking to her about her fire. He looked at me and said, "You again!" I said, "I had nothing to do with it."

I lived with my girlfriend for two years. Then I got a job. Fall of '83 with a local plumbing-supply company. I drove a truck for them and did counter sales. It was a good job. That lasted til '87. After I worked there, I went out to lunch one day, and I quit. I got bored, and I was drinking a lot back then. Just beer. From there, I went to this day labor hall. It used to be over on Broadway. I did general labor, industrial labor, and construction. At that point, I was living by myself in a cheap motel down on Sixth Avenue. It was called "the Paradise." I rented by the month—$250 or something a month. Back then, minimum wage was less than $4 an hour. I was making minimum and living at the Paradise. I worked for a machine shop for a while. I was using all kinds of hand grinders, grinding parts, taking the burrs off of aluminum and steel parts. I was also using this machine called a straight-liner machine, which put a sanded finish on all the parts before they got bent and painted. I worked for them for six months the first time . . . and quit there and went back to work for the day labor place again.

Most people think that people who are on the streets are lazy, or they don't want to work, or they can't work. There are a lot of people on the streets who have mental problems. Ever since Reagan opened up the doors to all the mental institutions and told everybody they could leave, a lot of people are on the streets who shouldn't be there. They're not all there mentally.

Once when I went down to apply for AHCCCS, I told them how much money I had been making for the past three months, working part-time out of this labor hall—averaged out to $337 dollars. They said the most I could make to qualify was $267 dollars a month. I thought they were discriminating against me because I was a white male. I thought that they thought that white males should make more money than that. I let the lady interviewing me know that I thought that was very arbitrary. The way the entitlement programs are, if you're an Anglo male, you don't really need this stuff; you're not supposed to be on welfare. But everyone is one paycheck away from being on the streets unless you got a whole bunch of money saved up.

My biggest challenge was the mistaken notion that I didn't have to have a whole bunch of money. Like I said, the "hippie thing" stuck: money isn't everything. I pounded it into my head so much, I'd look for excuses not to make a whole bunch of money. If I would have stayed with the post office, I'd be retired by now and have a big ol' house somewhere.

when i met **Lamanda Long,** she had recently been released from prison, where she had served two years for an illegal transfer of funds that had helped her young son receive a heart transplant. After her release, Lamanda stayed in Bethany House, a shelter for homeless women and children. A mother, a grandmother, and a certified public accountant with a master's degree in business administration, she had just found a job and an apartment when i interviewed her. she had also acquired legal guardianship of the seven children of one of her former inmates.

I was born in cleveland, ohio, March 22, 1955. I'm Indian, Irish, and black. I stayed in Cleveland until I was eighteen years old. I had two brothers, which were much older than I am. One of my brothers is ten years older, and the other one is fifteen years older.

I went to Jane Adams Vocational High School in Cleveland. I chose to go there. You had to basically be a 4- or 5-point average. I was always a 4.5 average. It was like goin' to college. I majored in legal secretary and minored in cake decorating. I also am a certified public accountant. I took those courses while I was in the service, and I have a master's degree in business administration from Case Western Reserve.

I joined the U.S. Air Force when I was nineteen. I served two years. Then I moved to California. In California, I worked for the engineering department of an automobile club. During that time, I was also a dance choreographer for several stage shows. My second job I worked in Vegas and Reno and Atlantic City. So I did a lot. As a teenager, I danced. I had a dance group called the Majestics. We danced all over Cleveland and New York—modern dance, modern jazz. We won awards for it. There were nine of us. I loved being a choreographer. It was an interesting, adventurous time in my life. I didn't have children then. I was in my twenties. My goodness, I did it up until I was twenty-five, and I had my baby. After he was born, I still danced until I was about twenty-nine.

When I turned thirty years old, I became very sick. I've always had a heart condition. I've had it ever since I was a child. I had rheumatic fever as a child. It scarred my heart. I had my first heart attack in the military. I was sick after that. My oldest son at that time was five or six. Also, he was very sick. He had problems with his lungs—fluid in his lungs. His lungs had collapsed. Also he had problems with his heart. It started when he was born and just continued.

My mother—she was alive then—used to pay for all of his medicine. His medicine was not covered through any state insurance [or] the private insurance I had; the medicine was so great in cost—I would say we spent anywhere from five hundred dollars to one thousand dollars a month in medicine alone. My mother died when I was thirty-five years old, and I think that's when everything went crazy. When my mother died, I could not afford the medicine. I couldn't get any help. I was living in Buena

Park, California. My mom died of cancer. She was diagnosed with having cancer one month and died eight months later. My son was also not doing well.

I did what any mother would do. I wanted to make sure my son had the medicine he needed to have. He also needed hospitalization during that time. I couldn't pay for that. I had Aetna insurance. Aetna insurance pays 80 percent of your bill. The other 20 percent ran into way over seventy-five thousand dollars. It was very high. I called the American Heart Association. I called the Lung Association. They said there was a waiting list. They were putting him on a waiting list! You don't have time for a waiting list when your son's in need, so I did my time for getting money to take care of my son basically. I guess I'd rather put it another way: to be able to keep my son alive, because he wouldn't be here today.

I knew when I did it, I'd go. I knew I was headed to prison. I believe that you get punished right here on earth for what you do. I'm very honest. I expected it. What I didn't expect was what happened with my kids. I didn't expect people to turn around and turn on you that have been with you all your life. I didn't expect people not to come and ask me, "Why?" I did not expect that. I learned a very hard lesson.

I was inside a little over two years. I was released January 28, 1999. I was here in Manzanita Unit [of the Arizona State Department of Corrections]. A lady from the prison ministries picked me up and took me to Bethany House, and that was hard. They were not expecting me. They told me I had to go through an intake. I had nothing but the clothes on my back. The room I shared was with two other women. They told me I had thirty days. They gave me some bus tickets. First they told me that I probably needed to train in some category of how to find a job. I explained to them I didn't need that because I'm very well educated, and I know how to find a job. I proved that by finding one in five days. I found this apartment in seven weeks.

The job is a document reviewer. I review documents for attorneys that are going to trial or to prepare them for trial. I found this apartment through Primavera Services. They gave me a list of apartments, and I basically did a lot of praying. I called two apartments and explained to the lady here my situation, and the manager was very nice. I came over and was able to get the apartment. Yes, they did need a security deposit.

Travelers Aid [a resource for homeless and near-homeless populations] paid for that. Their basic requirement was that you had to have a job and that you had children.

I have seven children, plus my own. They are four and a half months, three years old, nine, ten, thirteen, fourteen, and fifteen and a half. I have guardianship of all seven. I met their mother when I was in prison. At the time I met her, she was pregnant with [the youngest]. She was wondering what she was going to do with her children. She raised her children a certain way, just as I did. It touched me because my own children were divided up while I was doing my time. I have three of my own. Guess I really should say six because I have three stepchildren that I raised, too, and they were all affected.

I am a person that moves when God tells me to move, and for some reason he told me to offer my help. I saw that the children were having a lot of problems—also saw the environment they were in. They were in filth. The baby was laying in filth. I came home in tears.

I guess I've always had it in me to have other children in my home. If someone ran away, if a kid ran away, they ran to me. Even the counselors at the school knew that. They ran to me. I never turned a child away. I've kept siblings whose parents have walked off. I never put them in the system. I paid for them out of my own pocket. So I guess it's always been in me to do this. I just didn't know what my real calling was. Sometimes I even think going to prison was part of that. I had to see. So many women have the same problem. One of my goals is to help reunite some of these women with their children.

What made me take these children? This woman did for her kids basically what I did for mine. She had seven kids she couldn't feed. She got an abundance of food stamps she shouldn't have gotten to feed her children. If this shows you anything about our system: instead of the judge taking those children, taking her, giving her a social worker or giving her some sort of guidance, maybe even giving her a lot of community service and many years of probation, he sent her to prison for trying to feed her children. There's something wrong with that. This woman is serving seven and a half years. There are people who serve less time for pulling a gun and shooting someone. I see something wrong with the system.

I've seen so many women divided from their children. I've seen so many women whose children were put up for adoption while they were in prison. Some of them had only gone to prison for really minor things. You're only going to be there for four to five months. Things where maybe one judge would have just given probation, but this other judge gave them prison. When you wear a robe, you do as you want. That's basically it. Each one is different.

Some of the women are in there on charges that should not be there at all. I met a sixty-year-old woman who will be getting out next year. She's been in there thirty years. She's been in there for her husband trying to kill *her*. I think she got stabbed twelve times. She reached to hit him over the head with a lamp, and they gave her the time. She killed him, but she was stabbed twelve times. These women should not be there. She should not be getting out of prison at sixty years old. Her whole life's gone. She has five children, and I don't know how many grandchildren. And she has nowhere to go when she gets out. Her family has turned on her.

Women, on the whole, get more time than men. You could have a man with the same charge; he will get less time. He might get a slap on the hand and be told to go home. But not a woman. It's a status quo that women aren't supposed to be in trouble. They're not supposed to do things wrong. But society also has to realize that there are more single-women parents now. Whereas men a long time ago did things to feed their family, women are doing things to feed their families.

No one is perfect. There are a lot of mistakes made in this world. I made one. I made one in helping my children. There are a lot of officials and politicians who have made many mistakes in this world and are still acceptable, still on television. But when you're a normal citizen, and you make a mistake, it's not acceptable. You are actually the bad penny in society. It's very hard to clean that up.

delores johnson

barrio historico

I first saw **Delores** walking
in the barrio carrying a boom
box on her shoulder—a large,
striking, Native American
woman with painted purple
fingernails. I eventually
met her on a Saturday afternoon at the bus stop after she
had come from the liquor
store. We arranged to meet at
the "shrine" on Main Avenue
and Cushing Street, where she
and her "old man" would hang
out. Early one morning, we sat
on the adobe wall overlooking
votive candles, and later we
ate *carne asada* and tortillas
together.

My biggest challenge is surviving.

You don't know if you're gonna be alive when you wake up or if you're gonna be dead. You know? You just try to make the best of it—go day by day. I remember the first time I was on the streets, I was crying. I was scared—of any bug like that or things that crawled. I was terrified.

I've been homeless for years and years—since I was a little girl. I was born in Sells, Arizona, on the reservation, October 15, 1964. I'm Tohono O'odham and half Mexican. My mom was born in Sonora, Mexico. My dad was born in Sells. My grandparents were born in Sonora, and my dad's parents in Sells. My mom had to cross the border to get here—to the United States. That's what I heard, when she was young. The first reservation she got to was Sells, and that's how she met my dad.

I have six sisters and one brother. Growing up on the reservation was terrible 'cause there was no jobs for my mom. There was no food. My real dad and her had split up. They got a divorce. I was little, like three or four. My mom had met this other guy, and he was a Yaqui. He had found us a house on Tenth Avenue, at the old projects here in Tucson. When I talked to my real dad before he died, he was telling me that she messed around with another man. She locked us in the house, and she went to the bar. He told me we were all dirty. There was no food. My real dad passed away two years ago. He died of diabetes and alcohol, and my stepdad died of alcohol when I was thirteen years old.

My foster family was black. The first ones were black. The second ones were white. To me, when I was little, I'd rather be with them than be with my mother 'cause she did nothing but drink—all her life. I think that's why I'm an alcoholic today because I can't stop drinking. My mom drank because she was miserable. There was no money in the house, no food, and she loves to drink.

I was twelve when I started drinking. I started out with Budweiser. Then, I couldn't handle it. I remember running away. When we were in the foster home, she had got us back. That's when they found that house in the old projects where that church is now, but I didn't want to go back

there. I didn't stay too long with her 'cause my sisters were drinking. They introduced me to the beer, and then I started drinking.

I wasn't in school. The last grade I finished was sixth grade at Drachman School. I went to Carrillo School also. Carrillo was terrible 'cause the kids would fight us. The black kids, Mexicans, whites—they would fight us 'cause, I guess back then, they didn't like Indians, or they were trying to be tough or something. So we used to ditch school with my sisters. I'm the baby. There were six sisters, and three of them already died, and three of 'em are still alive. [One] died of alcohol, [one] died of leukemia, and [one] got in a car accident.

I think I was about thirteen when I first started living on the streets. I slept in the park. That park right there at the corner of 22nd Street. It's called Santa Rosa Park. I was by myself. Then I went to boarding school. They tried to send me to Sherman Indian High School in Riverside, California. I went. It was okay. At first I was crying 'cause I'd never been away from home. I was about fifteen. But it didn't work out 'cause I came right back. I mean, not right away, but I was doing terrible. I was into drinking, smoking weed, sniffing.

At the time all this stuff was going on, I wanted to kill myself. I was like on a suicide mission. I was miserable. I was very angry. I used to run away from my mom 'cause she was drinking. She wasn't even a mother. So I used to run away 'cause my mom used to drink and bring all her men friends. I got raped because of that, 'cause she used to gamble at the house right there. There was all of us girls. She would go to the bar and bring all these men back. And I got raped. I was little—about four. I still can remember it like it was yesterday. My mom said I wanted it—at four years old! She said I wanted it. She blamed it all on me. That's why I hate my mom. That's why we don't get along. I remember the last time she said, "You will be the first daughter to die because you're on the streets." Well, look, I'm alive. I'm still breathing. I'm here.

I've been in all kinds of rehab. I don't know why they don't work. I've been in Amity rehab for four years. I came back out and just started drinking. I thought it was going to work and everything. I guess I'm that kind of a person they say, "It'll work for some people, but not for all." I guess I'm the one person it wouldn't work for. I was sober there for four years. I was with my son at that time.

He's fourteen right now. I was nineteen when I had him. I was on the streets when I was pregnant. It was terrible, but I had to do it. I lived with him in an abandoned house. My son's a survivor, too. When he was born, we were both on the streets. He stays with my sister now. I had him here at the university hospital. After I had him, I asked my sister if I can live with her, so she says, "Yeah." Then after that, we got in a fight, and she kicked me out, so I went to live with my mom. After that got old, we got in a fight, and I was back on the streets.

It was tough. I was getting welfare checks and food stamps. I panhandled. Knowing you're a mother with a child, usually they would help you. If you're really going to buy food, they will help you. Me and him, we used to go house to house. Basically I didn't like it 'cause we were back to square one. When he was a baby, I was in transitional housing, but it didn't last long. It was just for a little while. Then I went to Rescue Mission with him. You sleep there and leave at five in the morning. You can't be drinking. You have to be sober.

Just talking about all of this, I need a beer. (Laughs.) The only thing I really needed in the whole time that I've been on the streets is a roof over my head because that's how they took my son away from me. My sister came and said that the judge gave her custody of my son without me signing no papers or nothing, so she like stole him from me. I think it was for his own good. Like I said, she didn't want him on the streets. She was trying to help me out and stuff like that—which I appreciated, you know.

But at the time I was mad 'cause that was the only son I got. She didn't do it the way I thought she would. She just, like, took him from me. I was mad! She was with this white lady from the [Tucson] Indian Center, so me and that lady got into a fight. At the time, they were trying to take my boy away from me 'cause I didn't have a roof over my head. That lady, she like grabbed his neck, and I grabbed her hair and yanked her out of her car. I just started fighting. My sister took him away. She had got papers, and she got it authorized. So she took him. . . . Now, we have a good relationship. I mean, he knows who's his mother. He knows that I have an alcoholic problem. He knows I'm homeless.

God has helped me survive. God and my strength and the people. You know, I panhandle. There's grouchy people. There's people who don't like homeless, but, you know, I still get something. They give me change or dollars or ten dollars. Usually I don't eat. I just drink. I don't care how it affects my diabetes. I love to drink. Nobody's gonna take my beer away from me. They've been trying for years and years. I keep coming back to it. From morning 'til ten o'clock in the nighttime, I could drink a lot of beer. I could drink four boxes in six hours—twelve packs in those boxes. I don't know where it all goes. But I'm still here.

This is my church right here. Yeah. I pray to the shrine. If [my old man] was here with me, we'd be drinking right here 'cause we've lost all kinds of people, you know. And we're on the streets. Where else can you go? I met [him] from his brother. I used to go out with his brother, but he died. They're all dying. He died of cirrhosis of the liver, drugs, pot—life! (Laughs.) I met him from his sister, and she died. They killed her. Some jerk killed her. Stabbed her ninety-nine times in the heart, cut her breasts off, sliced her face. I can't tell you who. She met this guy in a bar. He was crazy. He killed her with her own knife 'cause she used to carry a knife in her boot. Yeah, I knew her, and then I met her brother, and her brother was cute, and I fell in love. Then I met [my old man]. He used to go with my sister, and I used to go with his brother. Now, I'm goin' with him. (Laughs.) He's nice. Yeah, I love him. I want a man in my life. One that's gonna relate to me. I think [he's] the one that's relating to me 'cause we both drink. You know, we do things together.

I like this old Delores. I know I'm talking like I'm old. You know what I mean. I feel old. Yeah, 'cause of the diabetes and the alcohol. I feel like I'm 190 years old already. But when I'm drinking, I feel like I'm back to 13 years old. I feel young and purty. (Laughs.) Young and purty.

samuel is a can collector and pushes his "buggy" for miles each day. He can be seen heading to the Greyhound bus station, the attorneys' offices, the Transamerica building, or Presidio park, where he stations himself near the hot-dog lady. since 1991, he has helped her clean up in exchange for leftover dogs and coke. sam is always moving, constantly reaching into public waste receptacles, crunching cans, and exchanging greetings. He used to live in a house he filled with thousands of empty aluminum cans, while he slept on the porch. Now he lives in the corner of a warehouse that stores cappuccino carts, where he claims to be the "night watchman."

presidio park

I was born september 15, 1903,

in Morris, Kansas, Wyandotte Reservation. I had three brothers and one sister. They're all deceased—the whole family. I'm the only one left. Father was born in Guadalajara. His name was Roberto Martínez. My mother's name was Maria Beatrice Shaw. She was Sioux Indian. My mother was born in Guthrie, Oklahoma. She was real light with sandy hair. My grandmother was born somewhere—I don't know if it was Germany—somewhere out there. Years ago, I had a record, but they threw it away. I got ten different tribes in me. I got Chinese, Japanese, Hungarian, Warsaw, Aztec, Buffalo, Sioux, Tomahawk, Mohawk, and Cherryhawk. That's it.

I come from slavery people—from mixed people. When the slavery started, they didn't know who was who when they lived back in the cave. That's what they tell me. When they gather them all up, round 'em all up, see, like when you round up horses, you get mixed horses: brown ones, black ones, yellow ones, white, and maroon. Heh? That's the way they did the slaves over there.

I lived on a farm 'til about eighteen. I enjoyed the farm—walking the field, picking up the beans, and gatherin' the vegetables. I picked cotton in Oklahoma. There were only three farms: Chihuahua, Kansas, and Oklahoma. . . . I had good parents. I got spankings. When they tell you something, they mean it. See, Grandma'd take a hairbrush and work on you. And uncles, they take a fan belt and make a paddle, and that's what they spank you with. Not only me—their kids, too.

At eighteen, I went to St. Joseph's, Missouri. I went to O'Bryant School in St. Joe. We stayed there, and then we went to Detroit, Michigan. In Detroit, I stayed with my mother's sister. I went to school there. In 1918, I went to conservatory school. It was a Russian school. I know a little Croatian and Polish. I went to school in Kansas and Oklahoma, too. See, I had folks in Oklahoma, Kansas, and El Paso. I had full grandparents over in Chihuahua and Guadalajara, sisters and brothers there, too.

I stayed on a chicken farm in Kansas City, Kansas. I sold chicken and eggs in Kansas and St. Joseph's, Missouri. Turkey. I sold turkeys, sure, when I was in the chicken 'n' egg business. Turkeys. Yeah. Ginnies. I sold anything that got them ol' claw toes on it. Grandmother said, "They'll eat 'em." Ya' know? They'll eat 'em. See, my uncle was working in a flour mill, and mother was doing day work.

I stayed in a home in Detroit, too, until I got old enough. When I got twenty-one, I could go out and look for myself. I jobbed around in different places. Then I went back to school and went to anatomical school in college. That was free work. I was learning the trade. I worked at grocery stores, drug stores, Walgreen's in Chicago. In Detroit, I worked at the airport loading mailbags. I worked for Safeway, put things on the shelf and cleaned the backroom, got rid of junk. I worked on the Rock Island Railroad, Pullman porter in Chicago. I made the berths in Chicago and Omaha. I was just looking for work, running here and there. I saved my money and then go and divide it with my parents and grandparents.

Then I went to a sugar-beet farm in Eerie, Michigan. That's a slavery farm. I picked 'em. I was working on production. They were about the size of a watermelon, thirty-five to forty pounds. The seeds were scarce. Picked *fresas* [strawberries] and beans, too. I was working pretty good. I was making $995 a week. You worked up there. You didn't play. You worked. I made good, and then I went to Nogales to a girl named Locka Juana. That's a Spanish Indian name. It was back during Depression time. We were just friends. I went seeing some kids she helped raise. I helped raise all them kids—twenty-six children, thirteen girls and thirteen boys. Their parents starved to death. Old ones died then, during the Depression. So that's about all I can tell you.

I was married three times. All of them passed, too. Alicia—I met her in Mexico City at the airport. She was a ticket agent. She was in her thirties when we got married. She was older than I was. And Cuca. She's from Chihuahua. I met Cuca around '43, during wartime. The third wife, she was from Little Rock; that's all I can tell you. I can't tell you how old she was. I didn't keep her very long. Maybe six months. She was a good-time people, spent money.

I was put here in Tucson from the sugar beet in Eerie, Michigan. See, there's more of my people out here than there are down there. They're thicker here than in Kansas. See, the reservation was small. They moved to Eerie, a long ways. I can't tell you how many kilometers. They moved a long ways. I come out here, and I been here ever since. I enjoy it.

I'm the day watchman right here in this park. When I first started, I was looking for license numbers. Yeah. Out-of-date. I caught forty-four car thieves. I caught three sets of dope peddlers right here. Right here, I caught three sets of dope peddlers. I caught a man right down the street there. They were looking for him for forty-five years. I caught him. I got a man in the court up here. I caught him with a gun in the Supreme Court. I got another building here. I found two four-million-dollar payroll checks in the trash. I didn't cash 'em. I turned them in to the Bank of America. They belong to the government. You can't cash that kind of stuff. See, I belong to the reservation. I can't cash it. I'm still with the reservation—Wyandotte. I'm still on the books.

I go and get my cans. That's how I make my living. That's how I get my extra cash. I don't get paid. I'm working here free. I've been collecting cans for sixteen years, ever since I've been here. I started the first year I come here. Right now, times are kind of hard. Back in the '30s, things were hard. Times are hard right now, too. See, people are not drinking the pop like they used to. . . . I take my cans wherever the ad is. You sell them by the pound. When I first came here, it was eighty-five cents a pound—when I first come here. Then it went down all the way to eighteen cents a pound. No, I didn't sell 'em. I kept 'em in my house. I kept them all over: dining room, kitchen, bathroom. Made no difference 'cause nobody there but me. I had two tons of cans.

I put my profit in the bank, so you don't have to pay taxes on it. Everything I done, I look at my bank book and see what I made a year. I know how much profit I made when I turn it in. I itemize it. Sure. Then you send it to the IRS. But, I don't pay no income tax. I'm Indian, and they cut that out.

I get up at four o'clock in the morning. I wash my face and hands, comb my hair, get ready, and go buy my breakfast. Some mornings, I don't go eat 'cause I don't have the money. Have to go find my cans first. Go sell 'em, then come back. I eat right down the street on Stone. I get potatoes and tortillas. A lot of that takes the place of meat. I don't like a whole lotta meat. Meat is not good for you. Meat's got rickets in 'em. That's worms. Yeah, didn't you know that? Meat is not healthy for you. Snakes, rabbits, coons, deer, bear—I don't eat that kind of stuff.

I cook and eat out. Oh, I like fried potatoes and corn cakes. Tortillas—that's corn cakes. Beans, spaghetti and macaroni, tomatoes, onions, cabbage, greens, variety of greens, and variety of fruit. I go to the doctor every ninety days. I go next month for a checkup. I gotta get my teeth fixed. I only got seven teeth. Yeah, that's all. I don't drink, and I don't smoke. No tobacco and no alcohol. I've always been that way. I don't like to be around people when they're smokin' and drinkin'. And when I had a house, I didn't allow no smokin' or drinkin' in the house.

I leave here at 3:30 P.M., and I go home. I head back. It takes me about an hour. My buggy is heavy—weighs about four hundred pounds. I've got about a mile to walk. I night-watch over there at the coffee shop. I night-watch over there. I just watch the shop. I used to mop up, but I quit moppin'. I don't sweep. I've been there ten years.

When I get home, I put my coffee pot on. Wash my clothes at night, dry 'em, hang 'em up, and then change clothes. Put some more on, fresh the next day. Take a bath three times a week. Yeah. Wednesday and Saturday. I take another bath because I go to church on Sunday morning. I get up early enough, take a bath Sunday morning before I go to church. I'm used to it. That's the way grandmother used to wash us. I still have the same idea. That's what water is for.

I read the newspaper—the *New York Times,* the *Pittsburgh Courier,* the *Detroit Free Press,* the *Chicago Tribune*—and the Bible. The newspaper and the Bible, in Spanish and Jewish. I understand a little of four languages— enough to carry me through: Jewish, Spanish, Indian, English, and a little German. My grandmother spoke Sioux, German, and Spanish. I go to the Catholic church, but I'm Jewish. I go every Sunday and Monday to church—Guadalupe on 36th Street.

I talk to my people every day. I talk about different things, what happened years ago—that's all. Every day, I enjoy talking to 'em. I talk to them right here in the park, and a lot of people look at me. There's forty-six of 'em up there. I got aunts, uncles, brothers, sisters, grandparents, and cousins. They inform and advise me. Yeah, they're with me now. They're hollerin'. They're not talkin' to me. They're laughin' and talkin' and enjoying themselves. Sounds funny. But that's the way it is.

In five years, I'll be one hundred years old. I'm ninety-five now. What I know is when my time come, just be ready. That's all I can tell you. My parents always said, "When your time come, be ready." That's all. I don't plan on nothing. I'm liable to walk out on the street now, and some fool'll run up on me on the curb. Let's see. About four years ago, we had over three people killed right over there. Right over there. People run up on the curb and smashed them. See, drunk drivers.

I got nothing else to tell. Naw, that's it.

Deanna has cerulean blue eyes, dark blonde hair, and no front teeth. She is a thirty-six-year-old grandmother who has worked as a waitress, landscaper, drug dealer, and prostitute. Although she has a camp on the desert with a tent, fireplace, and solar shower, she often sleeps anywhere in town. I met her on a Monday morning when she was using the shower and laundry at Casa Paloma, a shelter for homeless women. Restless and jittery, Deanna smoked several cigarettes during her interview. Afterward, she showed me color snapshots of herself, years earlier, when she says she was "on top of the world."

deanna gillingham

casa paloma

Home? Huh? My mom's or my daughter's.

That would be my home. Can't live with my daughter 'cuz she's a doper. It's a smoke house—constant traffic all the time. I really don't have a home. Well, my mom's, you know, that's home, but I just don't live there. My stepfather and I don't get along. He molested my daughter years ago when she was eleven. I was in Pennsylvania at the time. They said [my daughter] made mountains out of a molehill. I had her put under hypnosis. Everything came out that he did. And my mom feels that 'cuz he went to counseling, he paid for it—that it's okay. You know what I'm sayin'? She forgave him. Really, she stays married to him 'cuz she wants that insurance money when he's gone. That's all she is, is money hungry. Dysfunctional. Dysfunctional family.

I was born in Clearfield, Pennsylvania, in 1963. I have three sisters, an alcoholic father. My mom and dad got divorced like when I was eight. Yeah, he used to beat my mom bad. Take him to jail. My mom's not a drinker. My dad was an alcoholic. He built my little sister and me a walk-in closet. We used to go in there when they'd be fighting. We'd go hide in this closet. We'd come out. The house'd be torn up. There'd be blood everywhere. It was just a bad scene.

He's the one who got me drinkin' when I was eight years old, yeah, 'cuz my mom would work. My mom worked in nursing homes as a nurse's aide. My dad was a tree surgeon—cut down apple trees, peach trees, oak trees. That's what he was. We grew up in bars, me and my little sister. That's where we were all the time. Yeah. He would sneak us shots. My sister would never drink it. He'd say, "Straighten' up! Be more like your father!" I was supposed to be his boy. He treated me like his boy, just roughhousing me and stuff. "Gotta be tough to be a drunk!" he'd say. He'd give me a shot of whiskey, and I'd drink it. We'd go pass out in the back in one of the booths. That's how my dad died—of liver failure. That's why I got it. I got cirrhosis already.

I got three kids—twenty, seventeen, and fourteen. And three grandkids—three, four and one. My son's at my mom's. He works. He's seventeen. He's got a landscaping job. He quit school when he was sixteen. My twenty-year-old has a house, but, like I said, she has twenty people livin' up there, stayin' up there, smokin' crack. I can't handle it with my grandkids there. CPS [Child Protective Services] is tryin' to take 'em, so I think she's settlin' down. I think she's straight'nin' up a little bit. She has three kids. Lazy ol' man who don't wanna work.

My fourteen-year-old's locked up. She kept having problems with my mom. She ran away. They took her to a rehab 'cuz she was smokin' crack—a rehab up north. She come back down here. They put her in a home. She kept runnin' from the home. Now they're thinkin' about takin' her to Vision Quest. They take 'em out in the country, you know, survival things. It's a home for troubled kids. She's been in rehab since January 1. Now she's in Juvenile Hall. No, I don't see her. CPS won't let me. She's in the system. The state owns her now.

I worked to support my family. I had construction jobs. I worked at the CAP [Central Arizona Project] plant out here. That's the water system they got out here. Watered down the dirt piles for ten dollars an hour, keep the dust down. That was only a four-month job. Then I did waitressin' at Johnny's Restaurant, Waffle House, and the Kettle. I was real good at waitressin'. Back home, I did work in the woods, runnin' a skidder, chain saws, cuttin' down trees. A skidder drags the trees out. You wrap the trees with chokers. There's six chains. You wrap 'em. Push the gas, and they come in, and you take 'em out.

I was maybe twenty-seven then. I had gone back 'n' forth from Tucson to Pennsylvania. After I left the father of my last two kids, I ended up with another guy for about six years. Then we split up. Then I got with that guy that died. He's the one who knocked my teeth out. I had partials. We were drinkin', fightin', drivin' down the road. He smacked me. My partial went flyin', so I went to grab it. He grabbed it and scrunched it. The main reason I'm out here is all because of alcohol.

It's not hard to become homeless. Once you get out there, it's hard to get back on top of things. A lot of it has to do with drugs and alcohol. Once you get on the streets, you become an addict or a drunk. Then you go downhill more and more from there. There is not really a lot of help. There's a lot of shelters for abused women, but not for homeless women.

I'm clean. I'm HIV negative. I go every three months to COPASA [Cooperative Outreach Project on AIDS in Southern Arizona] on south Sixth [Avenue]. Oh, yeah, I'm concerned. Most women on the streets are having unsafe sex. There needs to be more outreach. Most women don't care. They don't take the time out. Most homeless women get with homeless men. Most of 'em [the men], I feel, won't tell you if they're HIV positive, and they won't go through the trouble of using a condom. They're more concerned about getting their rocks off or takin' care of their own self. They don't think about what the consequences are gonna be.

Someone can always tell you, "Hell, I'm not HIV positive. I'm clean." A lot of 'em probably lie. That is a crime—to have sex with a woman knowing you have HIV. That's a crime most people won't admit to. Yeah. I had one friend die of HIV. A man. I sleep with him, and after I sleep with him, he tells me he's HIV positive, so that's how I got involved with COPASA.

I was workin' the streets. It's not a fun situation. You feel like two inches tall. You feel like a piece of meat, and there's so many weirdos out there. Just happened to me walkin' down the street one day. A guy says, "You need a ride?" And I said, "Sure." He wanted sex, and I said, "Yeah, two hundred dollars." That's how it happened. See, I've never been arrested for it. They have vice cops now. First offense for prostitution is ten days, right off the bat. I've never gone with a cop. They look like average people. You can't tell. They used to say, well, if you ask 'em if [they're] a cop, they have to tell you. But now they don't. The way to find out is you have to ask them to touch you. If they don't want to touch you, you know that's a cop.

Right now, I just don't know where to turn. I want to get my life together, but it's hard to work and be on the streets. I'm afraid I'm dyin'. Yeah, I know I'm dyin', you know. If I keep it up, I'm not gonna live to see forty—drinkin', smokin' pot, smokin' crack. I haven't smoked crack in a long time. That was a problem for a little while. I was in jail for sellin' an eight ball to a state cop, so I did my six months in Clearfield County Jail in Pennsylvania, which was the best thing that could've happen' to me 'cuz I was doing so much dope. Went down to eighty-six pounds. It was no fun bein' locked up, but it saved my life.

Last June and July I was on life support for twenty-two days from drinkin'. It was touch 'n go. Didn't think I was going to make it. I woke up one day, had tubes in me. I was in there almost all of June and July. Got laid up in this park. Called the ambulance once 'cuz my hands were real swelled. A bunch of my friends were drinkin' and stuff. I said, "I'm calling an ambulance. My hands are killing me!" So I went to the hospital. They knocked me out all night. Woke up the next day, and they told me, "You have gout." It's usually in your feet. That's what they told me. They gave me a bunch of pills and stuff.

Got out of the hospital after that night. I went up to the park, and I started taking these pills and drinkin', not eatin'. I guess I laid up there for three days bleedin' out of my nose. I was in a semicoma. Bleeding out of my nose and my mouth, and my friends said, "Oh, we'll pull you in the shade. We'll set you up and give you water." Well, after the third day, they finally called the hospital and the ambulance. That's when I went on life support. If I hadn't made it when I did, I would have been dead.

I have hepatitis A and B, and cirrhosis—only 30 percent of my liver left. Then they wanted to take out my gallbladder. I said, "Naw, you ain't takin' somethin' out that ain't broke." I don't know. They said my gallbladder was bad, but I'm not in pain or anything.

I dream of getting my family back together, having a normal life. Have my daughter. Do things with my grandkids like go to ball games. Go to parks, circuses. Just a normal life. It's the way a lot of people live.

Glenn Kiyota is a fifty-year-old japanese american who lives in his ford pickup. He has an iron-frame bed, stove, books, lantern, blankets, a three-month food supply, and a big-horn sheep skull inside the camper, and a bicycle rigged on top. After working several months in Tucson and saving three thousand dollars, he was heading up to Alaska and eventually to siberia. A small, wiry man with a pony tail and one tooth, Kiyota grew up in Hono-lulu, where he spoke japanese and chinese, and later learned German and Russian while in the army.

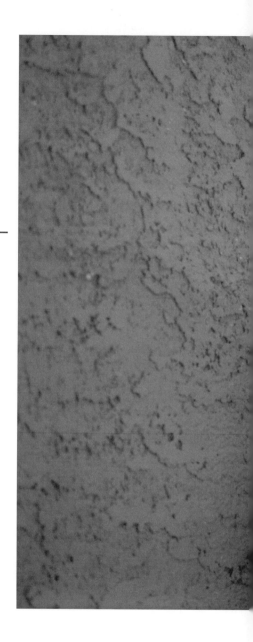

glenn kiyota

primavera works

I don't think I qualify

for being homeless. I don't think so. I'm never really homeless—homeless only to an extent that I don't have a house or an apartment. Home is wherever I park my truck or wherever I stop for the night. If I had to pinpoint one thing that's allowed me to survive, it's my attitude. I enjoy my kind of lifestyle.

I lived on the street twenty to twenty-five years ago just as an experiment to see what living on the street felt like. This was in Indiana, Pennsylvania. This was a small town. It's a college town. So I decided to do my own experiment. I lived one year on the streets— winter, spring, summer, and fall. Seven foot of snow in the winter. I slept in alleyways, abandoned houses. I had a lot of blankets, a lot of coats and clothes. If you actually haven't done it, you don't know the feeling of living on the streets. It's very stressful, but I knew I wasn't going to do this my whole life. It was just an experiment.

I learned a lot that year. You have to know how to survive, how to get along with people. You are always worrying about where your next meal is coming, where you'll be

sleeping that night, whether it's going to be cold or rainy, or whether you may be attacked, beat up, or thrown in jail. I learned also that I was very healthy, probably because of hereditary reasons. Now I've experienced Wyoming kind of weather, up in the northwest country, wind and cold. What makes a difference is the wind. I was in a small town living between buildings. As long as you have some kind of windbreak, a person can be comfortable, as far as not freezing.

About the first of June, I'll be heading back up towards Wyoming, Idaho, Montana, where I can go fishing. I can see wild animals—deer, moose, black bear, grizzly bear, hawks, eagles, squirrels. Anytime you're thirsty, you can stop by and dip your hand into a stream, a river, a creek and drink from it. But mostly up in the mountains where I'm away from people. I'm very good with people, but at the same time because I know people, I hate 'em. (Laughs.) I hate everything about people. If I depended on people, I'd be so stressed out I'd be in a mental ward or mental institution, whereas if I'm out in the wild by myself, there is only one person to blame if I don't make it, and that's me.

So far, I've been doin' this since 1981. The only reason I'm here in Tucson is because I drove down from Idaho and decided, "Well, I've never done the 'snowbird' trip." Yes, I'm snowbirding for the first time because I've heard a lot about snowbirders—good and bad. It's my first time in Tucson. First time as a "snowbird."

My ultimate goal is Alaska and Siberia. I've never been to Alaska, and Siberia because I would complete my goals that I set when I was thirteen years old: to see the world. I've been just about all over. I've been all over England, Europe, Germany, and free countries. Going to Alaska and Siberia will be one of my last goals. When I complete Siberia, if I ever do, then I'll settle down, get married, raise a family. My greatest challenge is to make it to Siberia because I'm probably going to have to be a wetback. More than likely I'm going to have to sneak in because although they allow traveling in Siberia, it's mainly done on a tour basis. You're escorted by people. I'm not the type to travel with a group of people. Like people coming in from Mexico, I'm going to have to sneak in.

I was born in Hawaii in 1949. My grandparents came from Japan. They migrated to Hawaii before the Second World War. I was brought up as a kid to live in the big city, like any kid at that time. You were taught: "Go to school. Graduate from high school. Go to college. Serve your military duty. Get married. Have kids. Buy a new house. Stay on the job. Stick to that job until you retire." At thirteen, I already knew what I wanted to do, which was to travel. I knew exactly what I was going to be doing as far as my goals in life, which was to travel the world, see the world, different sights, different foods and cultural experiences.

It wasn't until I got out of the military, serving time in Germany, that I started forming my opinions about society. My first serious thinking was about social security and retirement. I was selling real estate at that time in Des Moines, Iowa, and I dealt with a lot of old and retired people. I found throughout my experience that when you do get old, you may have all kinds of money, but healthwise, by the time you reach retirement age, you can't do nothin'.

Most of the people that I came across couldn't do anything because of health reasons: broken legs, broken hips, sickness. My philosophy on retirement and the "Golden Age" is that I'm taking my retirement *right now* on the installment basis. I work so many months. I make so much money. Then I take off so many months or so many years because when I do get old, I don't think I can do what I'm doing now, which is a lot of outdoors things—hiking, fishing, just throwing a sleeping bag over my back, and taking a can of pork 'n beans, and just go out into the wilderness for three or four days.

I climbed Mt. Whitney back in '82 in the summertime, by myself, which is very easy. There are trails all the way up. Oh, it was beautiful. In fact, Mt. Whitney is the highest point in the lower forty-eight. Not counting Alaska. Colorado has a lot of fourteen-footers. They've got one that's about fifteen thousand. But Mt. Whitney's about a few hundred feet, like five hundred feet taller than Pike's Peak. There are trails leading all the way up and down. Wherever a person goes in the United States, I don't see how people can get lost because there are roads all over the place.

I'm the type of person when I go traveling or am in transit, for example, if I see a road or a mountain or a rock or tree that's maybe a mile up the road, if I think it's interesting, I follow that road wherever it ends up. Could end up fifty miles down the road or five hundred miles down the road.

I traveled five years with donkeys. The only thing I owned were a pack and four donkeys. I started that trip back in June of 1985, along the Arizona–New Mexico line. There's a fence, a border fence at Old Mexico. I touched the fence and said, "I'm starting." I'd never been on a horse before or knew what a pack saddle looked like. Didn't know the first thing about packing. I didn't know how to ride a horse or put a saddle on a horse. I didn't know the first thing about surviving out there in the wild.

I picked up a book to see what a saddle looks like, how your things are supposed to be packed. I made most of the gear I carried on my four donkeys. I didn't even know how to treat a donkey, what they ate. They eat hay, but hay is such a broad term. Dried up leaves become hay if it has to. I was walking with all my belongings on these donkeys. I was heading north, going toward Alaska again, always north.

I was on that trip for five years. It took me about five years to get from the Old Mexico line to a place called Delta, Colorado. It's only a few hundred miles from where I started, but it took me five years because of the side trips I took. I didn't know the first thing about surviving in the outdoors. That's when I learned. So right now I can go anywhere in the world with just a knife and survive.

I was only six months into this traveling business with donkeys, and I came across the Gila River. In the month of April, it's already melting. The water is ice cold and high. We came to this crossing where we have to cross the river or else we have to backtrack fifty miles. So it took me an hour just looking into the water, staring into the water. Couldn't see the bottom because it was moving about fifteen to twenty miles an hour—green water and about forty foot across to the other side. Because I couldn't see the bottom, I kept staring and trying to decide, "What should I do?" Finally I said, "Well, you know, we're at the very bottom of New Mexico, and we have a long ways to go to the Canadian border. We're going to be crossing a lot more rivers, so we gotta try this one."

Finally I got the last donkey into the water—kept pulling on her—and at first the water was ankle deep, then knee deep, then thigh deep, then waist deep. The water was going twenty miles an hour, and it was about thirty degrees. When it got to the middle of the river, there was a big hole. It was so deep I couldn't touch bottom. It covered my head. I'm soakin' wet. I'm swimming. The donkeys are swimming, too, and I'm pulling. They're pulling down and panicking.

Finally we make it across, but one of the donkeys decided she ain't gonna do it. She stayed on the other side. All animals have a lead animal. I thought they would all follow, but this one decided to stay back. So I started walking up further, and eventually she did come. I'm telling the story because I was new at this. You should have faith in your animals to do what they're expected to do. They all made it. Everything got wet: cigarettes, food, everything. But I learned. I almost got washed away that time.

When the time is right, I'll head north to Alaska—stop in Montana and Wyoming on the way. Or I may stay there the rest of my life. . . . My parents are still alive, all in Hawaii. I'm the black sheep. I'm the only one who likes to travel or go away. Once in a great while, every couple years, I give them a call to let them know that I'm alive, and they always ask the same question, "When are you coming back?" My answer is always the same, "I don't have time because I have so many things that I gotta get done before I do retire." Which is true to a certain extent.

　　If I really wanted to, all I would have to do is find a job and be like regular people. Find a job, five-day work week, slave like everybody else does. Again, that's not my lifestyle.

vivian corbett

primavera works

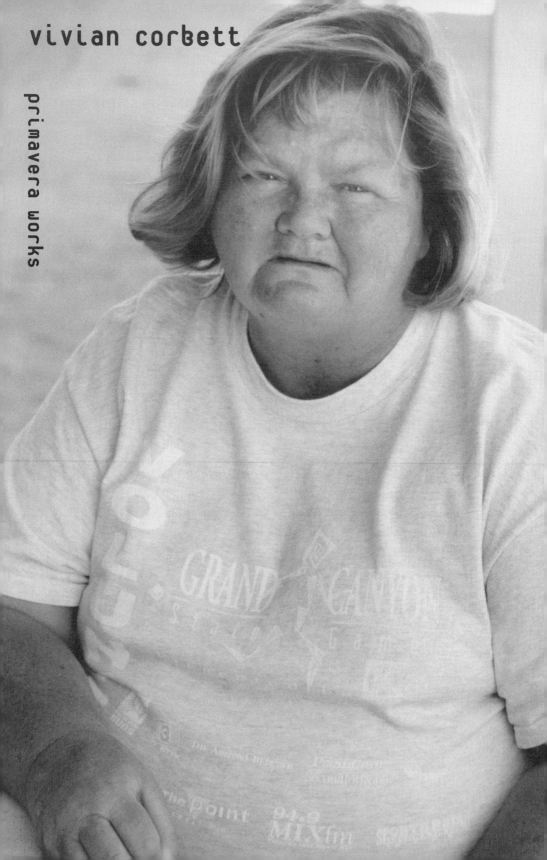

I met **vivian corbett** during her lunch hour between her morning job in the kitchen of the men's shelter on benson highway and her afternoon job on the cleanup crew for primavera services. After more than twenty years of living on the streets, vivian had recently found a home—a small trailer for $225 a month in rent. A mother and a grandmother, she said she was no longer in touch with her family and misses them very much. Before I left, she asked if I ever heard the birds sing at four a.m. and if I knew the hearty flavor of "hobo stew."

yes, I do. I have a little trailer.

I just recently moved into a bigger one from a small one. It's not the Waldorf Astoria. (Laughs.) It's just a little bigger. It's got a little living room. It's got a kitchen. It has one and half bedrooms and a bathroom. It's really nice coming from the streets to a place. I've been on the streets on and off since 1977—mostly on the streets.

You know what? Many nights I've slept outside with a knife next to my head not knowing if I'm going to wake up the next day. When I got in this little trailer, it felt so good to know that I don't have to worry about that—that I can feel that I can sleep and live again. That was part of my problem of being insecure. No home. No place to live. In order to really look at myself and see what I can do, you know? If you have a home, you do it better.

Now, I'm on the way up. I'm only doing the best I can. Through the help of Primavera, I'm good. They recognized me as a real person. That's exactly how they treat me here. They make me feel like a real person, so I must be a real person. So here I am. My life is probably not as complicated as some people's stories. It was hard enough for me. It's not easy outside when you're by yourself. I was a loner, you know.

Yeah. I was born in Stockton, California, in 1942. I'm German and English—a duke's mixture I guess. (Laughs.) I have one sister and three brothers. My father worked as a longshoreman for many years, and my mother was a housewife. I came from a dysfunctional family—a lot of fighting, a lot of drinking. My father had a problem with drinking. Later on, he had a mental problem. He tried to commit suicide several times, and I happened to have been there. I remember blood on the ceiling and things like this. I wasn't very old. 'Bout eight I guess.

I think because of that I married at a very early age. I was always going to school as a nervous wreck as a child because of my family problems. I never did finish the eighth grade. I just married so I could get out of it all. I married a boy that I was raised up with—grew up in the same

neighborhood. He was about four years older than me. I got married at fifteen and had two children by him. That only lasted about two years.

It was pure hell because we were not ready for marriage. I was still a kid. But, anyway, I ended up going into a mental institution after a nervous breakdown. They wouldn't let me go home to my own family because of too much disruption, too many problems. I was about eighteen I think. I had my family on one side of me and my mother-in-law across the way. My husband's car was always parked down at an ex-girlfriend's house. I guess I felt he was going out on me, and my mother-in-law was telling me how to live. Too many problems coming in on me at one time, and I blew it.

I had to go to the hospital, and they helped me with therapy. I had electric shock treatments because of depression, I believe. I remember trying to take my life once or twice. My husband claimed that I was incapable of taking care of my children, which was really not true. To me, I think I was capable of taking care of them. I wasn't mentally ill. I had an emotional problem. They never really said that I had a mental illness, you know. My children were still living with my husband, and I was given visiting rights. To this day, I really don't have much communication with any of them. I don't know where they are. We lost contact. It's hard for me to live with everyday because I really love my kids. I don't care how old they are. I really miss them with my heart, you know.

I've had five kids. I had [the last one] out of wedlock. It just happened. I don't know. I don't know where any of the kids are. It's like lack of communication, I guess. I know that I do have two grandchildren from [my youngest]. I did see them. They were darling. They're beautiful.

I gave up my children. That was half of my life right there. It was hard to go without my kids after having 'em since babies. It seemed like every time I turned around I was falling down, not being able to take care of myself. It's just been hard to survive for me out on the streets, trying to take care of myself. I went for years out here by myself, trying find this job and that job. I remember going in and out of restaurants asking to wash dishes or clean up the yard or anything to get a few bucks. It was a period of straight survival—not knowing who I can trust or nothin'.

I started drinking. I just started going to bars and drinking, kind of not giving a damn, 'til one day I just kept drinking and drinking and drinking and getting in more trouble and more trouble. Falling in the gutters, sleeping, drinking wine, not giving a damn. Giving up on life.

My biggest challenge in my life is just trying to survive as an individual. When I first got on the streets, I was over at Guadalupe Soup Kitchen, and I did run into an Indian man there. He was a nice guy. We got acquainted and started going together. He took care of me for a long time. He was really nice. We got along well. He was Navajo and Apache, one of the best friends I could ever have. I fell really in love with that guy.

We were living together. We had a couple of camp places. One was by the railroad tracks behind a big bush. Another one was down by the cab company, down close to Fourth Avenue. We'd always go there at night. I was very happy with him. He didn't want a house. He just wanted to live out, but he was good to me. I took him the way he was. Later on, he passed away in 1988. Well, he had a drinking problem, too. He laid down in Santa Rita Park and died before I could get to him. When that happened, I went crazy.

Friends told me that he died. Oh my God, I just screamed. That was terrible. And I had his Indian papers. I finally got a hold of the mortuary and was able to contact his family. Right now, he's buried in a little town called Tonalea. It's on the Indian reservation—the Navajo Reservation. I know where he is. I was told he was buried behind a church. It just seemed like I had his spirit walkin' with me even after he was gone.

I had to go on with my life. I went on and tried to be as happy as I could, except the fact is he's gone. He won't be back. That was a hard adjustment 'cause I really loved [him]. He was a sweetheart. My main thing was trying to survive on the street and how to take care of myself. The hard thing was trying to make something out of myself and fight alcohol at the same time. I found out that having alcohol in your life is just going to bring you down. I had to get rid of the alcohol before I could do anything with me. I've seen too many people die—my Indian friends. I've seen a lot of people die—even my mother and my father, too.

I was sitting in the park one day, and I guess I just cried out to God, "Help me!" and I think he did 'cause in a few days after that I ended up in LARC [Local Alcohol Rehabilitation Center]. I don't know how I got there. That's an alcoholic rehabilitation center. I let the alcohol go, and I haven't had a drink since. That's been close to eight years. It's my determination and my will keeping me sober today 'cause I've seen too much with my own eyes. I'm not going to let it kill me.

I would like to add that I know what it's like to walk down the street with nothing but the shirt on your back. I know what it's like to hurt inside. (Sighs.) I know what it's like to not have no money to the point where you're gonna do things that you have to do to survive. I sold my body a few times when I had to. I started resorting to crime—ripping things off from the grocery stores.

I got caught ripping off food. I used to eat cold pizza or KFC—all kinds of food people throw out in the dumper. In the back of the grocery stores, there's old vegetables, tomatoes. If you're hungry, you're going to eat it. I'd make sure it was clean. I had a big coffee can. I would find these steaks, cut 'em up, put in potatoes, and make a stew. I'd burn a fire by the railroad tracks—steak and potatoes and a can of beans. It's not bad. Hobo stew. Comes out pretty darn good.

Anything I had to do to survive is what I did. You know, there's not always a way out. People say there's a way out if you really want it. I don't think so. Not every time. The thing that keeps me going now is knowing that there is a reason for me to still be here. 'Cause I'm here. Believe in yourself, and you could move mountains if you really want to.

jon paul ferlan

magpies pizza

I met **jonnie,** a handsome, young "gutter punk," as he was limping down fourth avenue on a sunny january afternoon. someone had smashed his knee with a log on new year's eve, but he said he was too drunk that night to remember it. He was carrying a duffle bag that contained all of his belongings: a down comforter, *north-west guide to wildflowers,* crowbar, bondage chain and neck collar, a piece of twine, two mystery novels, and a porno magazine. although he did not smell bad, he said he had not taken a shower in six weeks.

I'm a gutter punk.

The hippies and ravers are like the more mellow people with a laid-back attitude. The gutter punks are the kids who like to fight and wear certain clothing. It's a more violent lifestyle than the kids who travel. The rainbows and the long-haired-type kids have more of a lifestyle they've chosen. They've taken the car that they had and what savings they have, and they move out to travel, where gutter punks are street kids—frustrated, angry runaways who grew up on the streets and ended up fighting and scrapping a lot.

I was born in Baton Rouge, Louisiana, in 1976. My father was Cajun, I believe, and my mother was White Mountain Apache. By my father, I have close to twenty-two brothers and sisters, I think, including me. By my mother, I have a sister. I haven't seen my dad since I was six. I haven't really wanted to. He was in prison for a while. Almost all twenty-two of his children filed sexual complaints against him. I found this out from my mother. He's a sick puppy. I remember a few instances of physical abuse. I still have curved ribs from when I was kicked across the room and slammed into a wall. I still remember that.

My mother was a junkie. One time I broke into my files and read all my paperwork. It was reported that I was neglected and stuff like that. When I was like a year and a couple months, I was taken to the hospital because I had turned blue and stopped breathing. I was pronounced dead, and they

tried to bring me back. They found I had been given drugs. They said they found that I had been given LSD at a party, according to the Child Protective Services report.

My mother abandoned me, and they transferred me on a plane to Tucson to Casa de los Niños [a shelter for abused and neglected children]. Then I stayed in a foster home on the South Side for two or three years. I remember that family. I did not like it. The kids there were sexually abusive to me. I was the youngest there. The foster parents didn't allow us toys because it brought jealousy between me and the other kids. There really wasn't much to do. I had to go to school, which I didn't like. I never liked school. I liked books, and I liked reading, so I would steal books from school.

Then I got adopted when I was about nine by a very rich family. They had a bunch of bunny rabbits and dogs. They were upper middle class. They got like a multimillion dollar home, something like that. I mean, to me that's rich. My dad was a stockbroker. I had two older siblings. One was two years older than me, and one was ten years older.

There were a lot of problems because they're pretty much normal people, and I was a very "damaged goods" type of kid—a lot of trouble for people who were used to having normal children. I'd, like, stash food. I wasn't close to people. When they would try to touch me, I'd shy away. I'd withdraw and read my books. I was very antisocial with a lot of emotional problems, like bed-wetting. My adoptive parents were unable of coping with my behaviors. I had a sullen attitude. I'd do what they told me, but I was verbally disrespectful. I was never violent. I got the impression my mother was a little neurotic perhaps and had expectations. My lack of response to her emotionally was painful for her.

I lived with them until I was eleven or twelve. From there, I was in institutions and lockup facilities 'til I was seventeen, mostly mental institutions and behavioral institutions, boot camp–type stuff. Anasazi, Adventure Discovery, Desert Hills. I was also in a day program that closed down a couple years because of sexual assaults by the staff, misdiagnoses, wrongful evaluations, and administering the wrong drugs for the wrong reasons. My psychologist for two years there tried to pick me up and take me to his house to watch movies with him and do dirty stuff.

I ended up being [in that program] for two years. My diagnoses varied. I was diagnosed as codependent, sociopath, bipolar, passive aggressive—a zillion different diagnoses. I had schizophrenic tendencies, suicidal tendencies, homicidal, blah, blah, blah. I was on something like fifteen different medications in two years. They kept switching me from doctor to doctor, ward to ward, because they couldn't figure out what was wrong with me.

The only medication I take now is alcohol. I feel better than I ever did then. When you have people on meds, they don't have any coping skills. You're numbed. You can't adapt when you're numb. I used to be a numb kid until I was nineteen. Then I fell in love and started growing emotionally. I was with my ex-fiancée. We shot dope for about a year and traveled around the country. Found out she was pregnant, got off the streets and stuff. I kicked heroin. We both were using. I kicked dope within one week of finding out she was pregnant. Within one week, I had found a job, got myself off the street—cold turkey.

We went twenty-four hours a day and seven days a week, two and a half years together. It's a lot of time. We lost the baby at four and half months. She had complications or something and miscarried. It was pretty horrible because I had hopes of being a father and starting a life. I had something I knew that would demand something more from me than I would demand of myself. A lot of times, I can be happy struggling. Being needed is a good thing sometimes because it puts things into focus.

After she lost the baby, we stayed together for a year and a couple months after that. Then on Christmas Eve, I fell off a ladder and busted my knee. We were fighting and arguing, and the stress was too much. She didn't want me to come back, so I became homeless again. I've been living on the streets—this last time—for about a year and a couple months. I find construction sites, condemned buildings, and sewers—stuff like that—to sleep in.

My greatest challenge has been the baby—kicking dope and losing the baby. My biggest fear is not getting off the street again, not getting my shit together again. That and becoming crazy. Like letting go. Like it's hard to believe when you've been living on the street, the way I have, that if you do A, then B will happen, and if you do B, C will happen. That's not really how life works most of the time. But you have to believe that in order to follow through with action. . . . I have just amazingly bad luck. You make your own luck to a certain degree. It's the little things—like falling off a ladder after I worked so hard. It's kind of a disheartening experience.

I've been in Tucson right now for about a month and a half. On an average day, I hang out in the park, get fronted some marijuana, and sell it for enough to go buy some alcohol. Or spare change for alcohol. Get drunk, usually vodka. I'm not much into beer. It gets me grumpy and fuzzy-headed. I used to drink every day. Now I drink four days out of the week. At night, I hang out and drink, try to go to punk rock shows or just obnoxious music in any form—heavy metal, rock, noise, ska, blues, jazz . . . anything but country. Any show that's cheap and under five bucks, I go to.

Yeah, my dream is to run around the rest of the world, fuck around like Henry Miller. Write a book. Have children. Maybe become a teacher. . . . When I was shooting heroin with my ex-fiancée and traveling the country, that was a best time, Henry Miller–type experience. I'm actually traveling with my girlfriend right now. She's also homeless. She's eighteen—the youngest girl I've been with.

I talk to other kids all the time. They're like, "Oh, umm . . . " They're not having safe sex. To some people, it's a casual joke even. "Yeah, I dumped my girlfriend. Let her know she's got B and C." Somebody said that the other day. I was like, "Oh, great." Hep [hepatitis] B and hep C. He's like, "Oh, I don't want to see you anymore. You're pregnant. And by the way, you have hep B and C." It's disturbing, but it's like real. HIV and AIDS is a concern. I don't do IV drugs anymore, although I still have sex. I like to keep one partner. You know? That's important to me. I don't like a lot of casual encounters. They're not rewarding, for me anyways. I'm kind of a single-minded person in that respect.

The reason we have a lot of our problems these days is because people used to have connections between generations. You'd have the grand-parents teaching the grandchildren. You know what I mean? A lot of societal roles and traditions. Things would be passed back and forth both ways. That doesn't happen anymore. Most homeless people are the very old and the very young.

I think that's why American culture is having a lot of social break-downs. Homelessness has more to do with social problems than it has to do with economic problems. Economics can always be fixed. We have plenty of resources here. It's not about the resources. It's about the interaction. You know what I mean?

I met **sweet forgetfulness** (margherita Abruzzo) on a sunday morning. she was sitting on a bench across from the wig store downtown eating pretzels out of a small plastic bag. she smelled of urine, had long dirty finger-nails, and was wearing a brown felt hat. she reminded me of a street gnome with a child's voice and curiosity. Having a conver-sation with her was like being in a maze of confusion, with moments of hard truth and poignancy spliced in. when I was getting ready to leave, she looked me right in the eye and said, "Ah, well, it's more than a story that's here."

"sweet forgetfulness"

congress and scott

I was born in France. Oh yes. Cupid's birthday. Valentine's Day is my birthday. I was born the year the cat crossed my path. I mean, to grow me took a lot of surgery and a lot of miracles. And my mom wasn't a survivor. Me and my dad went to Italy, and from Italy, we came to America. A long time ago. Well, see, they counted my age that many different times then when I got in school. They insisted to count my age on every graduation. So, actually right now I'm astronomical in the numbers of age according to the way they wanted me to count my age.

We had a big house. I can tell you what color it was. It changed when the wall came through. Actually, I'm famous all over the world, in the Eiffel Tower and everything. Well, when they came through and brought the wall through my home, anyhow. A government wall for animal gun law.

I was five when we came to America. We took something my dad designed to get here. Well, it was just kind of like at the instant surprise of the moment, you know on home invasion and brand new animal law control. My dad just got a hold of the right everything. My mother's not alive, but my dad is. Oh yes, he's here. He's everywhere I am. Poor guy. Isn't that piti-ful? (Laughs.) He lives his life. I live mine.

I studied English because I didn't speak it. I found it very interesting. I won't speak my language to anyone. As a matter of fact, I can practically write the English dictionary. Yeah, my godmother gave it to me for a graduation present. A dictionary. It's about that big. Every word in English. Well, this is more than a dic-tionary. This is the ultimate, maximum, translator, paper dictionary in English that anyone can get. I mean, that's what I read. That's what I write. That's what I translate. That's what I understand.

I'm French! I'm French! French-Italian-American. Well, the highest church of power in existence is the church I was raised in. Anyone can go to my church any day. I don't share my religion with anyone—just like my own language and my own name. I go to a tutor, a private tutor. Well, I've always had private tutors. I told you, I come from a very wealthy family. We never had to work until we came to America.

All my sisters' names? Well, we go by another name. Well, we had to get rebaptized and reconfirmed to enter this country, government, gun-controlled, animal-controlled world, and so we got new names when we got here. We're not really allowed to tell anybody our full names, like we're not even allowed to speak our own language.

I didn't like school forever either because of all the gun control. Well, you see, you go back to the original day-one million beginning. And, uh, did you hear all the news? You know? Guns kill. Guns don't protect. They kill. Did you hear the rest of the news? All your earnings from guns belong to someone else on the other side of the gun. And they're not yours, and they're not going to protect you.

Yeah, I worked in a grocery store, a bakery, and a bar and a restaurant and a clothing store and a jewelry store and a library. Now I don't have a job. I like not having a job. I've always taken the time to have my freedom because this isn't exactly the kind of world I like. Oh, holy God. Not really. This is the wrong world to fall in love 'cause it's not the name of the game.

Well, they kill legally every day. There are severe murders and killings every day. The world I'd like to live in, I'd never go there with any of these people. I'd go by myself. Exactly. I wouldn't even tell anyone. I still wouldn't tell anyone. Not a single word. It would be like me never mentioning my name or speaking my own language.

I gave up my home a long time ago. I gave up my home that many times because of people with guns. Yes, I've traveled all my life. I had a lot of things I really liked, and I gave them up for people with guns and gun control because the government's set up to legally, illegally kill people and kill 'em beyond all mercy. And when you've been through that many, passed through that many full aims and those kind of people, you don't trust anyone.

I believe in an eye for an eye and a tooth for a tooth. I've sacrificed everything I ever loved or cherished or wanted or had or desired or could've had. Just sacrificing and giving it up and having to sacrifice and give it up the way I had to and what it left me. I didn't give it to anyone that's going to get to keep it forever because they didn't get it in the kind of a way that they're going to keep it forever.

Well, I've outlived it. You might say I've kind of outlived all my greatest joys and greatest pleasures. My satisfaction is that everybody that's got everything I had to give up and give to them and had to live the life I had to live—because I had to do without to give it to them. Because of the way they chose that, they ain't gonna get to keep it. They're gonna get to lose it the same way. Only it's going to hurt them more than it ever hurt me. In the first place, it ain't theirs. In the second place, they've acquired it illegally and intended to keep it all illegally through an illegal, legal system.

So my greatest joy for years now has been going back to my dad. Going back to my whatchamacallit—my resource bank account, my process, returning and just counting the minutes and seconds of their future forever disappointment. Actually my dad couldn't think of a better way to break someone's heart. Well, he's just started breaking hearts.

I come from one of the wealthiest, holy-God-hell families in all of creation. There ain't nothin' that money can't buy. Yes, and I'm not worried. And yes, my dad's just started to break hearts. My grandparents were born on an island. We went down and insisted because my mother didn't survive. To pick up my grandparents on the way to this world. She died a horrible death—something like those dolls over there. Yeah, I was old enough to hear all the screams, old enough to know what happened. She's always with me now.

Actually, I throw them away. Yes. Oh God, I've thrown emeralds, rubies, diamonds, sapphires away. I always have. My mom and dad wouldn't know me if I didn't. Well, this is one of the most expensive stones in the world. It is the rarest. It's too expensive and too rare. It's only one of a kind! You should catch me on a mad day when I'm throwing jewelry around like crazy. It's like the shoe that don't fit.

All my worldly possessions are free to anyone and everyone. My home, all my home. Even my baby teeth are free. Yeah. My dad made my holy-God-hell baby teeth available. Well, it's a long story. It's in the future. Do you know Maximilian Schell? You don't know Maximilian Schell? That's right. You don't even know my dad, do you? You don't even know my history or my home or my circulation.

So where are brains made? Mastermind brains? Well, if your mastermind brain is an arsenal, a government-run arsenal to get away with murder and expecting that many benefits and that many returns and that many murders, that many possibilities, what do you think happens to a government like that? It self-destructs. But there's more to it than that. Oh yes.

Well, not for very long because the crazy people are all over the walls and doors when I get in—with their guns. They just won't leave me alone. I don't like to be inside really. I just can't forget those kind of guns breaking into my home, anyhow, on day one to begin with. Yes. The day I was born brand new.

So, did you get robbed? Did you get raped? Beaten? Imprisoned? Impounded? Not kidding, huh? Did they take your guns away from you? So anyway, how well do you know your guns? Well, how well do you know your enemies? How well do you know your friends?

Anne Frank was the sole survivor. We'll say day-one history knew her well. Well, basically she was a very wealthy girl, very intelligent and sole survivor and a victim of an insane, intelligent, illegal, legal-run government.

I was a survivor in this world because they made me a survivor. Now they're on the second half of the story. The ending. Yes. For every ending, there's a beginning. Do you know why for every ending, there's a beginning? Yes, well . . . I quit crying all my tears a long time ago. I quit screamin' all my screams a long time ago.

Ah, well, it's more than a story that's here.

steve Anton Kati is a fifty-year-old vietnam combat vet. A round-shaped guy with a thick moustache and sad eyes, steve was a little nervous when I met him one morning at **comin' home,** a residence for homeless vets on palo verde and Grant in Tucson. established ten years ago, **comin' home** houses thirty-eight veterans in two-bedroom apartments and treats them for a dual diagnosis: psychiatric disorder and substance abuse. steve has been coping with post-traumatic stress disorder and said he feels this is his "last chance" to get back on his feet.

steve anton kati

comin' home

Right now, I consider this home.

Would I be here if I didn't go to Vietnam? No, I don't think so because guys that I know from back home who didn't go, they went to work for Bendex. They're all retired now. I probably would have done the same thing. Probably wouldn't have been doin' the drugs. But the alcohol is pretty prevalent in my family. My father was an alcoholic. I never saw the man drunk, but that's because I probably never saw him sober. That's what it was. He was very functional and very stoic.

I was born in South Bend, Indiana, on approximately March 16, 1949. I was born at home, and then they took me to the hospital, and they chose that date I guess. My mother was born in Italy, and my father's Hungarian. They came to the United States in 1948. I have two older half-brothers who were born there, and I have a younger brother.

My childhood was terrible. My mother was very abusive. My father just worked really hard and was really not there for us. He worked for Studebakers, built cars. We lived in a small, two-bedroom house in a predominantly Hungarian neighborhood. I got up to about eighth grade. That's when I left home. It was a matter of survival. I had to leave. My mother was increasingly getting worse and worse. I think my mother's mentally ill. I think that's what it was, so I just left.

I was hanging out at a gas station in South Bend with older guys. They finally said, "You're hangin' out here so much, you might as well go to work." So the guy that owned the station would throw me twenty bucks a week, and I would clean up the place. Then I turned fifteen, and he gave me a full-time job. Then I got a little SRO, single room for myself. It was above a dry-cleaning, donut shop down the street from where I worked on Mishawaka Avenue. It's basically when I started drinkin' a lot. I actually started when I was eleven—mostly beer then, and flavored vodkas were really popular, like cherry vodka, lemon vodka. Very sweet.

The day I turned eighteen is the day I went into the service. That was 1967. The greatest thing I probably ever did was going to Vietnam. At times I feel like I was lucky to do that. It was a rite of passage that a lot of people don't get to do—into manhood. I mean, I had to grow up real quick at age eighteen. I had to learn how to survive.

It was no fun. Seen a lot of people get hurt, people get killed. They were trying to kill us, so I had to do what I had to do, right or wrong. I don't know. I don't know if our government was right on the whole thing, now that I look back on it. There's things that I've done that I'm not proud of—that were necessary but I'm not necessarily proud of. But they're mine. I'm gonna hold onto them. I don't think they were right. I have to deal with that.

I got out of the service in 1970 and got married the day after I got out. I met her while I was at Fort Carsen, Colorado. It was somebody I met there. I was just twenty-one years old. Married her. I was out of the service, and that's when things started goin' wrong for me. I lost a sense of purpose. When I was in the service, I knew what I was doin'. I was in control of every situation. If something went wrong when I was in Vietnam, I could pinpoint what went wrong and why. I couldn't do that in civilian life.

At that time, in 1970, people just didn't like us Vietnam vets. The war was winding down, and the peace movement in the U.S. had taken hold. When I came home into Travis Air Force Base in California, there were protestors right outside the gate. We were called names. We were called "baby killers." We were discriminated against. I would go to a job to fill out the application, and it'd say "service," and I'd put that down, and they wouldn't hire me.

So I talked to my dad. He said, "Come back to South Bend, and I'll get you a job at the factory." So I packed up my wife and my kid. Yeah, my wife was pregnant with my oldest boy when I married her. So I went to work where my dad worked at Allied Products. I started hangin' out with a few other guys who were workin' there that were vets just like me. Started partying a lot, smokin' a lot of dope, goin' out to the bars. I'd leave my wife home all night alone. By this time, she was pregnant with another child. So, finally, that marriage just broke up.

From those years until 1980, I lived in a succession of houses with my friends. We smoked a lot of dope. We sold a lot of dope. We did whatever we wanted. At that time, I went to work for Bendex Corporation. I was a lead man on a break line. Made real good money and then annual layoff came around. I just happened to be over at my mom and dad's house when my aunt who lives out here came over. She asked me what I was doin'. Told her

I was laid off. She said, "Well, if you ever want to come out to Arizona, just come on out. You can stay with me."

So I just got on a plane and came out here. She bought me a car and stuff. I went to work and got hooked up with some guys, Vietnam vets again out here in Tucson. Wrecked the car, wrecked a car of hers. That was the first time that I went to the VA [Veterans Administration] hospital for drug treatment. My aunt knew the director at the time, and she put me in there for drug treatment 'cause I was doing cocaine and alcohol.

I was real angry. I was put in seclusion a lot. It didn't matter what it was. That's just the way I dealt with the problems, being angry. That's when they put a diagnosis of "borderline personality" on me. That was the earliest thing they put on Vietnam vets. Then it was a "syndrome"; now it's up to a "disorder." So they gave me a "borderline personality." The whole period from '80 until '89 was a succession of psychiatric admissions to the VA hospital here.

By this time, I had met another woman and got married. I met her from a guy I went through treatment with. I think it was '82 or '83. I was very physically abusive to her. Sometimes my wife would take me in or I would go to the VA. I would go because I felt like I was gonna' kill somebody or hurt somebody. Then Maureen and I split up, and I continued to stay drinkin'. That's when I first became homeless. It was about 1984.

When I felt like hurting somebody or myself, I'd go to the VA, and they'd put me on ward five, the psych ward. I felt safe there, comfortable, knew everybody, so I was pretty much taken care of. Then I went through treatment in 1986–87, alcohol treatment. In 1989, I went through treatment again. About that time, Primavera [Services] was just startin' up. I was sober, so they put me into their Five Points Program [transitional housing]. I was doin' real well. I worked at the Jack-in-the-Box down on south Sixth Avenue in the morning cleaning up. Then I got a job at Council House apartments on Tenth Street. That turned into a full-time job. I was a janitor. Everything was going real well. I was promoted, and I got an apartment there.

From 1989 to 1993, I worked there, had my own place, was making good money. . . . A new manager came in and fired me for insubordination. I was so stressed out. I was going to a private doctor, and he was just giving me so many Xanax and Valium. Then I hurt my back. . . . I was at

Primavera at the men's shelter about '97. Then I went out to the desert and built a bunker out on the desert, out by the prisons. I bought sandbags and shoveled it out, timbered it up. I felt better when I was isolated. I worked day labor. But I knew I was drinkin' too much, so I went to the va in March of last year and signed up to go through the treatment program.

I did a month there, and then I had to interview for here. Now the va's carrying my contract, paying my rent here because I'm not able to work, cwt [Compensated Work Therapy, a work therapy program run by the va medical center]. My rent here is $280 a month. I don't know where I'm gonna go after my contract's up here. They sent me to an eye doctor and found out I got glaucoma in my eye. All these health problems are comin' up. So, I don't know.

I don't think I would be in the position I am if I didn't go to Vietnam. No, I'm sure I wouldn't have the anger. I know I wouldn't have the nightmares. I wouldn't have the sleep disorder. I'm a diagnosed insomniac. I have to take medication just to go to sleep. I have to take medication for anxiety, [and] take medication for depression. This is the first time that I've actually got a good regimen of medication. I take Klonopin, which is like Valium, for anxiety. It's here. I can just come and sign for it when I need it. I can take it three times a day.

I'm a survivor. I'm able to take care of myself. It doesn't matter if I got thrown out of here today. I wouldn't worry about it. I'd pack up a little backpack, take bare necessities that I need to live on, and I could survive. My greatest challenge is right now—to get right back on to where I'm supposed to be. I mean, I'm fifty years old. I don't have anything. I got one pair of jeans. You know? In a moment's notice, I can be gone. My greatest challenge is not to leave here, to rough out this stuff.

Like I have a group tonight I really hate. I've been in so many groups. I've been in va hospitals so many times. But this time, I think I've set my mind on things. I think this is my last chance. Next Friday I go down to an adult education class, and I'm gonna get my GED. That was one of my goals. I'm doing it.

I would like to feel a sense of well-being in me, a good feeling just about myself. To *know* when it's happening and to recognize it: that I am good.

NATIONAL INFORMATION CENTERS

National Coalition for the Homeless
1012 14th Street NW, Suite 600
Washington, D.C. 20005-3406
phone: 202-737-6444
fax: 202-737-6445
website: www.nch.ari.net

National Alliance to End Homelessness
1518 K Street NW, Suite 206
Washington, D.C. 20005
phone: 202-638-1526
fax: 202-638-4664
e-mail: naehnaeh.org
website: www.endhomelessness.org

The Doe Fund
232 East 84th Street
New York, N.Y. 10028
phone: 212-628-5207
fax: 212-249-5589
website: www.doe.org

Founded in 1986 by George McDonald, the Doe Fund is named after a homeless woman whom McDonald fed in Grand Central Station and who died of pneumonia on a Christmas Day. The fund's programs include an employment program for homeless men, a computer-training lab, GED and literacy training, a residence for homeless people with AIDS, a single-room occupant (SRO) facility, and a project in central Harlem that helps women on welfare and female heads of households receive training and find work, and provides day care for their children.

TUCSON AGENCIES AND SERVICES

shelters for women and children
Bethany House (520-690-1295)
Salvation Army (520-622-5411)
Travelers Aid (520-622-8900)
Tucson Shalom House (520-325-8800)

shelters for men
Gospel Rescue Mission (520-622-3495)
Primavera Shelter (520-623-4300)
Salvation Army (520-622-5411)
Travelers Aid (520-622-8900)

shelters and services for youth
Open Inn (520-670-9040)
Our Town (520-323-1706)
Youth on Their Own (520-293-1136)

shelters for infants and children
Casa de los Niños (520-624-5600)

domestic violence centers
AVA (Assistance for Victims of Abuse) Shelter (520-795-4880)
Brewster Center (520-622-6347)
Casa Amparo (520-746-1501)
Tucson Centers for Women and Children (520-795-4266)

meals
Casa Maria (520-624-0312)
Gospel Rescue Mission (520-622-3495)
Caridad (520-623-6773)

Daytime Drop-ins
Primavera Relief and Referral (520-623-5111)
Toole Avenue Homeless Services (520-884-0707)
Casa Paloma, for women only (520-882-0820)

Employment opportunities
Dorothy Kret and Associates (520-790-7677)
Jackson Employment Center (520-882-5500)
Primavera WORKS (520-882-9668)
Primavera Employment Services (520-884-5244)

Health services
El Rio Health Center (520-670-3909): Homeless Health Care Project
Compass Health Care (520-624-5272): detox for men and women
Southern Arizona AIDS Foundation (SAAF) (520-628-7223): AIDS-related
    services
Cooperative Outreach Project on AIDS in Southern Arizona (COPASA) for
    Women (520-295-9339): HIV-education program for IV drug–using
    women
La Frontera Readily Accessible People Program (RAPP) (520-882-8422):
    outreach to homeless, seriously mentally ill (SMI) persons
Pima County Health Department (520-740-8613): TB testing, needle
    exchange
COPE Behavioral Services (520-884-0707): services for homeless SMI
    persons

Transitional Housing
Nosotros (520-623-3489): shelter for resident Tucson families
Pio Decimo Center (520-622-2801): transitional living for neighborhood
    families
Primavera Services (520-623-5111): transitional housing programs
Southern Arizona AIDS Foundation (SAAF) (520-628-7223): housing and
    services for people with AIDS

Tucson Metropolitan Ministries (TMM) Family Services (520-322-9557): transitional living for women and children

Travelers Aid (520-622-8900): a variety of services, both emergency and long range

Tucson Shalom House (520-325-8800): transitional living for women and children

veterans' services

Comin' Home (520-322-6980): transitional and supportive housing for veterans

Esperanza en Escalante (520-571-8294): veterans and their families transitional housing

VA Homeless Program (520-629-1839): support services for homeless vets

VA Supportive Housing (520-791-4739): housing contracted by the City of Tucson

Barbara Seyda received a B.S. degree from the University of Wisconsin–Madison and an M.F.A. degree from Rutgers University. In 1988, she became an assistant photo editor for Stewart, Tabori, and Chang on their twelve-volume series, *The Smithsonian Guide to Historic America*. In 1990, she was an assistant photo editor for *Elle* magazine, as well as a photojournalist and writer for *Outweek*. Her first book, *Women in Love: Portraits of Lesbian Mothers and Their Families*, was published by Bulfinch Press in 1998 and won a Lambda Literary Award. Her work has been published in *Ms., Essence*, the *San Francisco Examiner*, the *Advocate, Sojourner*, and many other publications. She has taught at Rutgers University, Pratt Institute, and the New School for Social Research. She is currently a freelance writer and photographer living in Tucson, Arizona.